Women Who Dared

52 Stories of Fearless Daredevils, Adventurers & Rebels

LINDA SKEERS

ILLUSTRATED BY LIVI GOSLING

sourcebooks
jabberwocky

Published by Sourcebooks
P.O. Box 4410, Naperville, Illinois 60567-4410
(630) 961-3900
sourcebooks.com

Library of Congress Cataloging-in-Publication Data is on file with the publisher.

Source of Production: PrintPlus Limited, Shenzhen, Guangdong Province, China
Date of Production: November 2020
Run Number: 5020375

Printed and bound in China.
PP 20 19 18 17 16 15 14 13 12

CONTENTS

DAREDEVILS

ANNA OLGA ALBERTINA BROWN
1858-1919(?) • GERMANY
SUPERIOR STRENGTH 1

ANNIE EDSON TAYLOR
1838-1921 • UNITED STATES
PLUNGING INTO PERIL 2

BESSIE COLEMAN
1892(?)-1926 • UNITED STATES
ACE AVIATOR 5

ELINOR SMITH
1911-2010 • UNITED STATES
FEARLESS FLYER 6

FLORENCE CHADWICK
1918-1995 • UNITED STATES
SENSATIONAL SWIMMER 9

GEORGIA "TINY" BROADWICK
1893-1978 • UNITED STATES
PETITE PARACHUTIST 10

HELEN GIBSON
1892-1977 • UNITED STATES
STUPENDOUS STUNTWOMAN 13

LILLIAN BOYER
1901-1989 • UNITED STATES
WING-WALKING WONDER 14

LILLIAN LEITZEL
1892-1931 • GERMANY
AWESOME ACROBAT 17

MARY LILLIAN ELLISON
1923-2007 • UNITED STATES
"FABULOUS MOOLAH" 18

MAY EMMELINE WIRTH
1894-1978 • AUSTRALIA
OUTRAGEOUS TRICK RIDER 21

MILDRED BURKE
1915-1989 • UNITED STATES
"QUEEN OF THE RING" 22

SHIRLEY MULDOWNEY
1940- • UNITED SATES
RAD RACER 25

SOPHIE BLANCHARD
1778-1819 • FRANCE
BRAVE BALLOONIST 26

VALENTINA TERESHKOVA
1937- • RUSSIA
COOL COSMONAUT 29

ADVENTURERS

ADA BLACKJACK
1898-1983 • UNITED STATES
ARCTIC SURVIVOR 33

BARBARA HILLARY
1931- • UNITED STATES
NORTH AND SOUTH POLE SENSATION 34

BEATRICE AYETTEY
1955- • GHANA
UNCONVENTIONAL CAPTAIN 37

EMMA "GRANDMA" GATEWOOD
1887-1973 • UNITED STATES
HIKER WITH HEART 38

DR. EUGENIE CLARK
1922-2015 • UNITED STATES
SHARK LADY 41

FANNY BULLOCK WORKMAN
1859-1925 • UNITED STATES
COURAGEOUS CLIMBER 42

FERMINIA SARRAS
1840-1915 • NICARAGUA
COPPER QUEEN 45

IDA LEWIS
1842-1911 • UNITED STATES
LIGHTHOUSE KEEPER AND LIFE SAVER 46

JEANNE BARET
1740-1807 • FRANCE
SECRET SAILOR 49

JOAN BAMFORD FLETCHER
1918-1979 • CANADA
REMARKABLE RESCUER 50

JUNKO TABEI
1939-2016 • JAPAN
MOUNTAINEERING MARVEL 53

LIBBY RIDDLES
1956- • UNITED STATES
MASTERFUL MUSHER 54

LILLIAN RIGGS
1888-1977 • UNITED STATES
REMARKABLE RANCHER 57

MARGARET BOURKE-WHITE
1904-1971 • UNITED STATES
FEARLESS PHOTOGRAPHER 58

MARY ANNING
1799-1847 • ENGLAND
FOSSIL FINDER AND DINOSAUR
DISCOVERER 61

MINA HUBBARD
1870-1956 • CANADA
EXCITING EXPLORER 62

ROSALY LOPES
1957- • BRAZIL
DARING DISCOVERER 65

SYLVIA EARLE
1935- • UNITED STATES
UNDERWATER WANDERER 66

YNES MEXIA
1870-1938 • UNITED STATES
BRAVE BOTANIST 69

REBELS

ALIA MUHAMMAD BAKER
1953- • IRAQ
LIONHEARTED LIBRARIAN 73

ANNETTE KELLERMAN
1887-1975 • AUSTRALIA
MERMAID QUEEN 74

ANNIE "LONDONDERRY" COHEN KOPCHOVSKY
1870-1947 • LATVIA
BODACIOUS BICYCLIST 77

BELLE BOYD
1844-1900 • UNITED STATES
SLY SPY 78

BESSIE STRINGFIELD
1911-1993 • JAMAICA
"MOTORCYCLE QUEEN OF MIAMI" 81

ELLA HATTAN
1859-1907(?) • UNITED STATES
QUEEN OF THE SWORD 82

IRENA SENDLER
1910-2008 • POLAND
HEROINE OF THE HOLOCAUST 85

JOHANNA JULY
1857(?)-1946(?) • MEXICO
HORSE WHISPERER 86

KATE WARNE
1833-1868 • UNITED STATES
DARING DETECTIVE 89

KEIKO FUKUDA
1913-2013 • JAPAN
AMAZING MARTIAL ARTIST 90

LYDA CONLEY
1869-1946 • UNITED STATES
PROUD PROTECTOR 93

MARGARET "MOLLY" TOBIN BROWN
1867-1932 • UNITED STATES
ABSOLUTELY "UNSINKABLE" 94

MARY EDWARDS WALKER
1832-1919 • UNITED STATES
MEDAL OF HONOR WINNER 97

MARY FIELDS
1832-1914 • UNITED STATES
STAGECOACH MARY 98

MINNIE SPOTTED WOLF
1923-1988 • UNITED STATES
MARVELOUS MARINE 101

ROSE FORTUNE
1774-1864 • UNITED STATES
COURAGEOUS COP 102

SUSAN LA FLESCHE PICOTTE
1865-1915 • UNITED STATES
HEROIC HEALER 105

SYBIL LUDINGTON
1761-1839 • UNITED STATES
HEROIC HORSEWOMAN 106

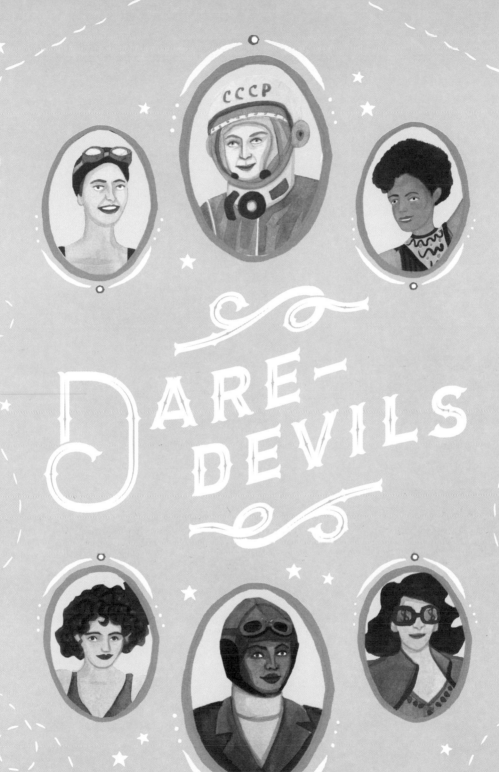

ANNA OLGA ALBERTINA BROWN

★ SUPERIOR STRENGTH ★

In the 1800s, circuses were a popular form of entertainment around the world. In 1858, two acrobats had a baby girl and named her Anna Olga Albertina Brown. It's not surprising that she joined the family business. From a young age she was an accomplished trapeze artist, tightrope walker, and gymnast.

Anna performed under the stage name "Miss La La." She was tiny—under five feet tall. Although she looked like a child, she had the strength of a grown man—a very STRONG man. And that's what set her apart from the other trapeze artists.

Being biracial also gave her an air of mystery, which publicists capitalized on when they released stories about her background before her appearances. Rumors were rampant before performances. The more outlandish the story, the more tickets were sold.

Anna's act was astonishing and unique. She'd start out by hanging a hook with a dangling leather strap over a trapeze bar. She'd then bite down on the strap and hang there by her teeth—and spin!

That was just the warm-up. She'd also hang by her knees from a trapeze bar while holding a leather strap connected to another trapeze bar in her teeth. But then, a child, a woman, and a man would hang on that trapeze bar!

By that point the audience would be amazed by her poise and strength. But there was more to come. Much more.

Anna would be lifted to the top of the circus tent, and with just one leg swung over a trapeze bar, this dainty acrobat in a ruffled skirt would hold three grown men aloft—one on each arm and one hanging onto a strap she held in her teeth.

Her big finale was a booming success—literally. She would lift a cannon attached to a leather strap into the air with her teeth, and then it would be FIRED! She'd be flung back from the blast—still clenching the cannon—earning her the nickname "Iron Jaw."

When she was twenty-one, Anna was immortalized in a painting by the famous French Impressionist artist Edgar Degas. He'd seen her perform several times in Montmarte, Paris, and wanted to capture her beauty, strength, and grace on canvas. The painting depicts her suspended from a rope attached to the roof of the circus tent—a rope she's holding in her teeth. The oil painting, *Miss La La at the Cirque Fernando*, hangs in the National Gallery in London. One art critic proclaimed it to be one of the artist's finest works. It certainly portrays one of the finest, strongest, and bravest women the circus has ever known!

ANNIE EDSON TAYLOR

★ PLUNGING INTO PERIL ★

In 1901, in the small town of Bay City, Michigan, Civil War widow Annie Taylor was thinking about retiring. For years, she'd been giving dance and etiquette lessons to children. But as she got older, the students stopped coming. She had no savings and wasn't interested in getting an ordinary job—she wanted fame and fortune!

She just didn't know how to get it.

One evening, she was reading a newspaper article about all the tourists flocking to see Niagara Falls. She decided to show them something far more exciting than waterfalls, something never seen before—the first person to go over the falls in a barrel!

An ordinary pickle barrel wouldn't do, so Annie designed one herself. It was made of white oak and reinforced with iron bands. A blacksmith's anvil was set in the bottom to keep the barrel upright. She would grip metal handles and be secured with leather straps.

Annie was ready to take the plunge but wanted to make sure people were there to watch. For weeks, newspapers and posters advertised "the fearless Mrs. Taylor" and her daring, death-defying stunt.

On October 24, 1901, on her sixty-third birthday, Annie rode to the falls in a carriage. Thousands had come out to witness the spectacle. She strapped herself in and crammed pillows around her. The barrel was sealed and fastened with screws.

People gasped as the barrel tumbled and tossed its way closer to the edge. The roaring of the Falls drowned out the excited and terrified roaring of the crowd as Annie went over and down!

At first, nothing could be seen in the swirling water. Then, Annie's barrel bobbed to the surface!

It floated to the shore, and workmen frantically sawed off the top of the barrel.

Annie slowly crawled out. She was bruised and battered, but ALIVE! The first thing she said was, "I prayed every second I was in the barrel except for a few seconds after the fall when I was unconscious."

Annie may not have made the fortune she'd hoped for, but she loved sharing her story.

She set up a souvenir stand near Niagara Falls and sold postcards and booklets about her life. The "queen of the falls" will go down in history as one fearless—and perhaps a bit reckless—daredevil.

ANNIE EDSON TAYLOR
HEROINE OF NIAGARA FALLS

BESSIE COLEMAN

★ ACE AVIATOR ★

Bessie Coleman was born in a tiny cabin in Texas, but even as a child she had big dreams. She picked cotton and helped wash and iron clothes, but she also attended school and excelled at math. When Bessie was eleven years old, something happened that caught her attention—and changed her life. The Wright Brothers flew their first plane! She read everything she could find about airplanes, dreaming about the day she would soar through the sky.

As a young woman, Bessie moved to Chicago, where her older brothers lived. She worked as a manicurist and saved money for flying lessons. She applied to flight school…and was rejected. She kept applying. And she kept getting rejected for the same two reasons—she was a woman and she was African-American.

Bessie refused to give up, so when she learned that women were being taught to fly in France, she knew what she had to do. She worked harder to save money and took classes to learn French!

Bessie sailed to Europe, and soon she was finally taking flying lessons. Even though she had to walk several miles each day to school and she witnessed fatal crashes, her desire to fly never wavered. Bessie even managed to graduate from the ten-month course in seven months. In 1921, she became the first African-American woman to earn an international pilot's license.

When she returned to the States, parades were held in her honor. Newspaper articles were written about her. She was a celebrity—a celebrity without a job. There were no aviation jobs for a woman. She returned to Europe and studied air acrobatics. Bessie returned to the States again—this time as a stunt pilot. She amazed thousands of spectators at her shows—doing loop-de-loops, figure eights, and barrel rolls.

The press nicknamed her "Queen Bess" and wrote about her breathtaking stunts. In 1925, the show didn't go as planned. She had a serious crash and broke several bones. But instead of being upset about her physical injuries, she was sad that she had disappointed the fans who had bought tickets to see her fly. A year later, she was back in the air.

As Bessie traveled the country, she frequently talked to young girls and women about aviation. She wanted to encourage and inspire the next generation to pursue their dreams of flying, just as she had. And that's exactly what she did.

ELINOR SMITH

★ FEARLESS FLYER ★

When Elinor was six years old, her family was driving through the country when they saw a sign that said AIRPLANE RIDES $5.00. Elinor and her little brother climbed into the cockpit, and off they went. Before the plane had even landed, Elinor knew she was born to fly!

She started taking flying lessons when she was ten. Since she was too short to reach the pedals, her instructor tied blocks of wood to them. She also sat on a pillow so she could see where she was headed.

In 1928, when she was only sixteen years old, Elinor became the youngest person to receive a pilot's license—signed by Orville Wright!

Elinor was an inspiration to other girls who wanted to fly. But not everyone believed in her—male pilots often teased and ridiculed her. One stunt pilot went even further and bet she wasn't good enough to fly under one of New York's bridges—something no one had ever done before. He expected her to back down and admit she wasn't capable. She didn't. Elinor not only accepted his dare, she said she would fly under all FOUR bridges in New York.

Elinor carefully prepared for this spectacular feat. She studied tides, measured, and calculated her route. On Sunday, October 21, 1928, the seventeen-year-old was ready. Before she took off, the legendary aviator Charles Lindbergh personally wished her luck.

Newsreel reporters lined the bridges as she took off. She flew under the Queensboro bridge, just feet above the river. Then she ducked her plane under the Williamsburg Bridge. Halfway done! She waved to spectators and swooped under the Manhattan Bridge.

Only the Brooklyn Bridge was left—but there was a problem. A tanker and a Navy ship were chugging away under the bridge. Would she fit? She turned her plane and flew sideways under the bridge and between the ships!

Her stunt played on newsreels in movie theaters all over the world. It also came to the attention of New York's mayor. What she had done was illegal. She could lose her pilot's license forever. Instead, it was suspended for ten days. Rather than being considered a criminal, she was hailed as a hero!

Elinor went on to set speed, altitude, and endurance records—too many for her to count. She also became the first woman test pilot for two airplane manufacturers.

Not only was Elinor born to fly, but she opened doors—and the skies—to future generations of female aviators!

FLORENCE CHADWICK

★ SENSATIONAL SWIMMER ★

Florence grew up in sunny San Diego, California and started taking swimming lessons when she was six years old. Before long, she was competing in swimming meets, and she won her first one when she was ten. But the smooth, still water in swimming pools didn't provide enough of a challenge. Florence was drawn to the rough, unpredictable nature of the ocean—that's where she felt the most at home. At ten, she was the youngest person to swim across the mouth of San Diego Bay.

Florence was always looking for her next challenge, and she set her sights on swimming the English Channel in record time.

It wouldn't be an easy feat—long endurance swims are unpredictable. Besides the currents, the cold temperatures, and the blowing winds, Florence could encounter seaweed, sunburn, stingrays, jellyfish, sharks, and debris. No two swims are ever the same.

In July 1950, she attempted to swim the English Channel.

She failed.

But she refused to give up on her dream.

A month later, on August 8, 1950, Florence tried again. She swam from France to England in thirteen hours, twenty minutes, breaking a speed record that had stood for twenty-four years. But she wasn't satisfied. A year later she swam the Channel again—from England to France—the first woman to swim the Channel both ways!

On July 4, 1952, Florence set a new goal: to swim between Catalina Island and the California coast, a twenty-one-mile stretch. Small boats surrounded her, frequently fending off sharks when they got too close to her. A thick fog rolled in, making it impossible for her to judge how close she was to the coastline. After almost sixteen hours in the water, exhausted and disoriented, Florence asked to be pulled into one of the boats. She was disheartened to realize she was less than a mile from the shore.

Never one to dwell on defeat, two months later she tried again. And again, a thick fog rolled in. But this time she ignored it and just kept swimming—and she succeeded!

Florence continued to find and conquer bodies of water all around the world, adding to her list of women's "firsts" in swimming. In 1970, she was inducted into the International Swimming Hall of Fame.

Florence is remembered as not only an amazing swimmer but also a woman with a fierce determination to set goals and do whatever it takes to achieve them.

GEORGIA "TINY" BROADWICK

★ PETITE PARACHUTIST ★

Georgia weighed only three pounds when she was born, which earned her the nickname "Tiny." Despite her size, she was fearless and active. At fifteen, she watched Charles Broadwick's World Famous Aeronauts parachute from a hot-air balloon. The dangerous stunt fascinated her, so she asked to join his troupe of performers. Not only did he agree, she became an important member of his skydiving family.

As a petite teenager, Georgia wore a silk dress, ruffled bloomers, and a bonnet and was promoted as the "Doll Girl." The nickname may have helped sell tickets but she always hated it. Georgia would sit on a trapeze bar suspended from a hot-air balloon and jump off and parachute to the ground.

In January 1912, the *Los Angeles Times* wrote about her daring jumps, and that caught the attention of a pilot who asked if she was ready for something more dramatic—parachuting out of a plane! She didn't hesitate.

Soaring high above the ground, Georgia crawled out of the cockpit and stood on the side of the biplane. She wore a bulky parachute attached to the plane by a static line. She stepped off into space, the line pulled the parachute open, and she floated to the ground—landing on her feet. She was the first woman to parachute from a plane—and she was just getting started!

Not all of Georgia's landings were on target. She landed on a windmill, in a swamp, in trees, on a roof, and on the top of a caboose as it rolled down the tracks. Despite broken bones, sprained ankles, bumps, and bruises, nothing could dampen the excitement over her next jump.

In 1914, the U.S. Army took an interest in her parachuting skills. In four successful jumps, she demonstrated how the parachute was deployed by a static line attached to the plane. But as she made her fifth jump, something went wrong! The cord got tangled, and she was left tossing and twirling under the plane as it flew. She stayed calm, quickly cut the static line, and deployed the parachute by hand—making her the first person to free-fall from a plane. Georgia was also the first to prove to the military that airmen could safely bail out of airplanes and live. This led to the invention of the ripcord, and it changed the way parachutes were packed and deployed from then on.

Georgia retired in 1922, after approximately 1,100 jumps. In 1964, she donated one of the silk parachutes she used—handmade by Charles Broadwick—to the Smithsonian Institute, at a dinner celebrating her legacy. She may have been tiny, but she had big dreams—and the passion and determination to achieve them!

HELEN GIBSON

★ STUPENDOUS STUNTWOMAN ★

Helen was working at a boring job in a cigar factory when she went to a Wild West show. It was an evening packed with excitement and thrills—something she wanted more of in her own life. She headed to a ranch in Oklahoma to learn to ride horses and soon excelled at trick riding. Helen performed in rodeos, but then a new form of entertainment popped up—movies! Helen was hired to ride horses in Westerns, earning fifteen dollars a week, which was a lot of money at that time.

She became the stuntwoman for the popular movie series, *The Hazards of Helen*. When the star got sick, Helen took over as the lead and did several episodes. It continued for years, with Helen doing stunts in sixty-nine of them.

Totally fearless, she tackled each stunt the writers came up with. One of her most dangerous ones had her driving a team of horses, detaching them from the wagon, standing on their backs, catching a rope hanging from a bridge, and swinging from the horses onto a moving train. She did it without getting hurt—but she *did* get a raise!

Helen became known as the first professional stuntwoman in Hollywood and was given her own movie series called *A Daughter of Daring*. And her stunts got even more daring. For one of her most famous scenes she practiced jumping from the roof of a train station onto a train while it was standing still. But when the cameras started rolling, so did the train! She jumped, landed, and rolled almost off the back of the train! Luckily, she grabbed onto an air vent at the last second. She then dangled over the edge, making the scene even more dramatic.

In 1924, Helen joined the Ringling Bros. and Barnum & Bailey circus as a trick rider. It was exciting, but not as exciting as doing movie stunts. After three years, she returned to Hollywood, trading her horses for motorcycles and even more incredible stunts!

One of her most impressive scenes involved riding a motorcycle onto a train platform, through the open door of a boxcar, and onto a flatcar—all while the train chugged down the tracks!

Helen's last appearance in a movie was in 1961, when she was sixty-nine years old. This amazing and talented daredevil not only led an adventurous life, but blazed a trail for other fearless stuntwomen to make their mark in both movies and television.

LILLIAN BOYER

★ WING-WALKING WONDER ★

When Lillian was in her early twenties, she worked as a waitress in Chicago. Two of her regular customers were barnstormers—airplane pilots who flew so low they skimmed the roofs of barns and did stunts for entertainment. It was the early days of flight, and the public was fascinated by aerial acrobatics. When the barnstormers asked Lillian to go for a ride in their open-cockpit biplane, she didn't hesitate. It was love at first flight!

A few days later Lillian went up again, but this time she wasn't content to just enjoy the scenery. She climbed out of the cockpit and walked back and forth on the wing!

Lillian left her waitressing days behind her and became a wing-walker performing in front of huge crowds at fairs and festivals all over the country and Canada. During her career, she stated many times that she never felt scared—even though she performed without safety gear or a parachute. She had complete trust in her partner, Billy Brock, a barnstormer and former World War I pilot.

Before attempting a trick in the air, Lillian practiced in a barn. She also trained to keep herself in top physical shape. Their act was called "Lillian Boyer's Flying Circus," and she did some of the most death-defying tricks of any of the daredevils of the day.

To begin her thirty-minute show, Lillian would stand on a speeding car as the plane swooped low over her. She'd grab onto a ladder and pull herself up onto the wing. Then she'd hang by one hand or dangle by her knees—the first woman daring enough to hang like that in midair.

Another thrilling trick involved Lillian sliding her feet into straps on the plane's wings. Then Billy would do loops in the air—hoping that the straps didn't break!

One of her most spectacular stunts was also the most dangerous. Lillian would crawl out of the cockpit and attach a thin cable to the wing's supporting bar. On the other end was a mouthpiece that she bit down on. Then, she'd slowly slide off the wing and hang by her teeth! Lillian also did parachute drops. Once, after jumping from the plane, she realized she was descending too close to a Ferris wheel. The operator stopped it just in time for her to land safely in one of its cars.

In 1928, federal flying regulations changed, putting an end to the dangerous sport of barnstorming. Even though "The Most Daring Girl in All the World" had her feet on the ground, she still captivated listeners with tales of her escapades in the air.

LILLIAN LEITZEL

★ AWESOME ACROBAT ★

Lillian was born into a family of circus performers. She was a good student and studied literature, music, and ballet. Her parents hoped she would be a concert pianist instead of a circus performer. But Lillian was determined to join the circus.

She practiced gymnastics and aerial acrobatics, and at fourteen, she joined her mother's female troupe. In 1910, they traveled to America and performed for the Barnum and Bailey Circus. The act didn't get the rave reviews they were hoping for, and they headed back to Europe. Except for Lillian—she stayed, determined to become a star.

Her billing, "Lillian Leitzel, the World's Foremost and Most Daring Aerial Star," was almost bigger than she was. She performed in a nightclub—hanging from a rope and doing poses, twirls, and spins. A scout for the Ringling Bros. Circus caught her act. The tiny aerialist with the big personality signed a contract and was on her way to stardom!

When the two circuses merged into the Ringling Bros. and Barnum & Bailey, she became their headliner—and stayed in that lofty position longer than anyone else. As their star, she had her own railroad car—complete with a baby grand piano!

Lillian's act was as dramatic as she was. The lights dimmed and she appeared in the glow of a spotlight. Not content to just climb the rope, she rolled and twirled her way up until she was fifty feet off the ground—with no safety net. Hanging by a pair of silver rings, she twirled, spun, and did breathtaking acrobatics.

The second part of her act featured her signature move. She slipped her wrist into a rope loop attached to a swivel. A drum roll began…all eyes focused on her. She would then swing her body around like a human propeller while cymbals crashed and the audience counted the turns. She was known for doing over 100 turns at a time—her record was 249!

As the act went on in a blur, Lillian's hair would slowly come undone, making it look like she was flying apart—and that was partially true. Each turn caused her shoulder to dislocate and then pop back into the socket.

Twenty-five years after her death, this "Queen of the Air" twirled her way into the International Circus Hall of Fame in 1958, a spot she earned as the "darling of the Big Top."

$ MARY LILLIAN ELLISON $

★ "FABULOUS MOOLAH" ★

Lillian, as she liked to be called, was born in South Carolina and spent her early childhood picking cotton and playing with her twelve older brothers. One night, her dad took her to a professional wrestling match. At that time, wrestling was more about acting and showmanship than athletic ability. It was a wild night of colorful characters and over-the-top action, and Lillian wanted to be a part of it! Her dad and brothers were against the idea of her becoming a lady wrestler—but when anyone told Lillian she couldn't do something, she was determined to prove them wrong.

And she did!

She started out as a valet, or ringside assistant, for a male wrestler known as the Elephant Boy. She would enter the ring, brush his hair to make it wild and bushy, and kiss him on the cheek. He'd grunt and growl and toss his opponent around.

But Lillian wasn't content to be anyone's valet. She wanted to be a wrestler, and a star! On May 26, 1949, she had her first match—a very boring match. She needed a gimmick, something to make people pay attention. When asked why she wanted to wrestle, Lillian had a sassy answer: "For the moolah!" That was when Lillian became the Fabulous Moolah!

She started getting more matches and quickly realized that crowds loved a villain, so she gave them what they wanted. Lillian used a lot of flashy—and not quite condoned—wrestling moves. Flying dropkicks, scissor holds, body slams—the more outrageous, the better. Her signature move was the "Moolah Whip." Lillian would grab her opponent's hair and whip her around the ring.

Lillian was also known to hide a pipe in her tights and take it out when the referee wasn't looking. She'd bonk her opponent with it and then hide it again. Soon the fans would be screaming wildly at the referee to disqualify her. But she wasn't done yet. She'd wave the pipe, let her opponent grab it, and then have the referee disqualify *her*!

Lillian didn't care if the fans cheered, booed, or called wrestling fake—just so they paid attention. And they did! The Fabulous Moolah held the title of Women's Championship of the World for almost thirty years—winning her last match when she was seventy-six. In 1995, she was the first woman inducted into the World Wrestling Entertainment (WWE) Hall of Fame. And "entertaining" sums her up perfectly!

MAY EMMELINE WIRTH

★ ★ OUTRAGEOUS TRICK RIDER ★

May grew up in Australia with her family of circus performers. As a child she was a tightrope walker, contortionist, and acrobat. But this pint-sized powerhouse was really born to ride!

By the time she was ten, she was a bareback trick riding star. In the audience for one performance was one of John Ringling's scouts looking for new talent. And when May did back somersaults from one galloping horse to another, he knew he had found it!

For two years she toured with the Barnum and Bailey circus in the United States. Crowds loved this smiling young equestrian in her signature pink bow. She was billed as "the world's greatest bareback rider" and was determined to prove it.

May wasn't content to do the same act for every show, so she was always creating new and more amazing—and dangerous—stunts. She somersaulted through rings—backwards. She knelt on the horse's back and then did a forward flip, landing gracefully upright. Then she tried something no one had ever attempted before. May stood on a galloping stallion facing its tail. Then she would somersault high in the air, spin, and land back on the horse facing forward!

May performed her trick routines while music played—and she occasionally danced the Charleston, a popular dance at the time, while standing on the horse's back as it galloped around the ring.

One of her more unusual tricks was also a crowd favorite. May would stand in the ring, but instead of shoes, she would have wicker baskets on her feet. She would then jump up onto the back of a galloping horse. To make it even harder, she would do this while wearing a blindfold!

May liked to boast that she could ride anything with four feet. One day a lawyer challenged her to prove it by riding his untamed prize bull, King Jess—bareback. A talented equestrian as daring as May was not about to back down from a dare! May not only rode the bull, but she did a handstand on its back!

May's trick riding career lasted over twenty-five years. As one of the most admired and beloved circus performers, she was inducted into the Circus Hall of Fame in 1964.

May was born to ride—and she did that better and more spectacularly than most!

MILDRED BURKE

★ "QUEEN OF THE RING" ★

Mildred was a young mother without a high school diploma working as a waitress. She needed a change, but what else could she do?

She went on a date to a pro-wrestling match, where she was one of the few women among thousands of men. Mildred was fascinated by the strength, power, and control of the wrestlers. She wanted try it—and asked a wrestling manager to train her. He refused. She kept asking. Finally, he told her he'd set up a match with an eighteen-year-old male wrestler. Mildred didn't know the wrestler had been told to body slam her so she'd stop pestering the manager.

But he didn't get the chance, because Mildred pinned *him*!

The manager asked for a rematch.

Mildred pinned the same wrestler again.

She was on her way to becoming one of the world's best lady wrestlers. Mildred took training very seriously: lifting weights, watching her diet, and exercising daily.

She started wrestling in carnivals. Her manager would offer $25 to anyone—male or female—who could pin her in ten minutes. Nobody could.

Mildred (or "Millie" as she liked to be called) was strong, but she was also smart. Science was her advantage—she used her opponents' own weight as leverage against them. She studied all types of moves and holds and practiced until she mastered them. Her signature move was the "alligator clutch," a speedy spinning maneuver that tied her opponent up like a pretzel! Mildred's quickness in the ring earned her the nickname the "Kansas Cyclone."

In 1936, she moved from the carnival circuit to sporting arenas. As her reputation grew, so did her fame. Newspapers and magazines wrote about her. Newsreels showed her wrestling by day in lots of makeup and going out at night in silk dresses and high heels. She wanted to prove that women could be successful athletes in a tough, male-dominated sport and still maintain their femininity.

All through her career, she encouraged women to try wrestling. In November 1954, she took a group of women wrestlers to Japan for several matches. At first, the Japanese were stunned—the idea of women wrestling shattered long-held traditions of proper female behavior. But slowly, they accepted the strength and grace of the sport. A year later the All Japan Women's Pro-Wrestling Association was formed!

After winning more than five thousand matches, Millie retired from the ring and became a trainer and manager. Her wrestlers were known as "Millie's Girls," and they continued to prove that women are quite capable of being "queens of the ring."

SHIRLEY MULDOWNEY

★ RAD RACER ★

Shirley's life has always been zooming along the fast track. She dropped out of high school and got married at sixteen. Her husband, Jack Muldowney, had a passion for cars—he built them, fixed them, and raced them. And after Shirley learned to drive, she discovered a love of racing too. At first, it was just for fun. But the more she raced, the more serious she became about the sport.

Drag racing usually takes place on a straight, quarter-mile track with two cars racing head to head. It's about fifteen seconds of excitement at speeds upwards of 250 miles per hour! When the cars zip past the finish line, a parachute shoots out the back of the car to help slow it down.

Shirley was the first woman to enter the world of professional drag racing. She received her license from the National Hot Rod Association in 1965. It was tough being a woman in a male-dominated sport. She found it almost impossible to find sponsors to help defray the costs involved. It was also hard to find crew members to work on her car. But Shirley refused to be intimidated or give up, and people changed their minds when she started winning, and winning, and winning!

Fans also loved her because she made quite a sight at race tracks. Her car was painted hot pink, which matched her pink uniform and helmet. She wanted people to know there was a woman racing! During her career, as she piled up wins, she gained respect and the nickname "The First Lady of Drag Racing."

But racing is a dangerous sport, and Shirley found that out the hard way. During a race in Montreal, Canada in 1984, a front tire tube snapped, her wheels locked up, and her car spun and somersaulted down the track. She survived—barely. Emergency personnel spent hours scrubbing her with wire brushes to remove the grease and grit from her skin before she could undergo surgery to repair her shattered legs, broken pelvis, and crushed fingers. Doctors weren't sure she would ever walk again—let alone drive a race car.

Two things happened after her accident: improvements were made to racing wheels and tires to make them safer; and Shirley surprised the doctors. Not only did she walk after several surgeries and eighteen months of grueling physical therapy, but she returned to racing in 1986!

Shirley was inducted into the International Drag Racing Hall of Fame in 2006 after a long—and speedy—career!

SOPHIE BLANCHARD

★ BRAVE BALLOONIST ★

By all accounts, Sophie was a shy, nervous, and skittish young girl. She didn't like loud noises or riding in horse-drawn carriages. And that makes her chosen profession even more surprising!

She married the much older Jean-Pierre Blanchard when she was just a teenager. He was a talented balloonist but a lousy businessman. He needed something new that would attract the ticket-buying public to help him pay off debts. He decided a *female* balloonist would draw big crowds, and Sophie agreed to give it a try. She made her first ascent in 1804 and fell in love. While Sophie was fearful on land, she was calm, bold, and fearless in the sky.

After Pierre's death, Sophie continued to put on demonstrations across Europe—even drifting over the Alps!

Ballooning was an incredibly dangerous endeavor at that time. A hot-air balloon has a fire that needs to be stoked constantly to keep the balloon aloft, so Sophie switched to a balloon powered by hydrogen gas. But that didn't lessen the danger. One wayward spark could turn the balloon into a blazing inferno. To Sophie, the thrill of ballooning and entertaining audiences was worth the risk. And using gas enabled her to fly higher, stay up longer, and kept her hands free. She loved flying at night—sometimes all night. She would attach parachutes to little baskets of fireworks and let them float down to the ground. Audiences loved the sizzling, flickering spectacle and the dainty and daring balloonist.

Sophie became such a beloved performer of Napoleon Bonaparte that he proclaimed her to be the "aeronaut of official festivals." She flew over his wedding reception, and when his son was born, she soared over Paris and dropped birth announcements to the people below. She also set off fireworks from her balloon for his baptism.

Several times, Sophie lost consciousness while ascending too high. Temperatures could be freezing, and one night she fell asleep in the balloon—and woke up with icicles on her hands and face. Another time she crash-landed in a marsh and nearly drowned before rescuers could pull her out.

Sophie bested the danger and defied social norms, stereotypes, and even gravity itself to prove that women could successfully achieve their high-flying dreams.

VALENTINA TERESHKOVA

★ COOL COSMONAUT ★

Valentina was born in 1937, in a poor village in central Russia where her parents had immigrated from Belarus. Her father died when she was just a toddler, and life was tough for her and her mother. But Valentina always looked to the sky—and forward to her future.

When she was twenty-two years old, Valentina took up skydiving. She loved it and had over 125 jumps to her name when she set her sights even higher. During this time, the United States and the Soviet Union were in an unofficial competition known as the "space race." Each country wanted to prove it had the most advanced space exploration program in the world. Each country one-upped the other to implement new technology and make its way into outer space.

Valentina was working in a textile mill but still wanted to do her part. She wrote to the Soviet Space Commission and asked if she could become a cosmonaut.

The odds were against her.

No women had ever been in the space program.

She had no scientific background.

She had no flight training.

But she was a skilled parachutist—and that helped Russian premier Nikita Khrushchev choose her for an intense, eighteen-month-long secret training session. Valentina learned to fly a jet and studied rocket theory and spacecraft engineering. There were also grueling physical challenges such as being spun in a centrifuge, enduring weightless flights, and long periods of isolation.

On June 16, 1963, when she was twenty-six years old, Valentina was shot into space in *Vostok* 6. During the launch she shouted, "Hey, sky, take off your hat! I'm coming to see you." Her radio name was Chaika, which is Russian for "seagull." It was fitting because she soared through space for over seventy hours—orbiting the earth forty-eight times! During her trip she took photos and kept a log of the effects of space flight on her body.

Besides airsickness, she faced two glitches during her mission. First, she forgot a toothbrush! She made do with toothpaste and her finger.

The second glitch was more serious. Valentina realized there was a problem with the control panel. If mission control couldn't fix the computer program, she wouldn't be able to return to Earth. Instead, she would have floated off into space…forever.

The problem was fixed, and she successfully ejected from the capsule four miles from the earth's surface.

Valentina was hailed as a national hero and proved that the sky is NOT the limit for a woman who has set her sights high!

ADVEN-TURERS

ADA BLACKJACK

★ ARCTIC SURVIVOR ★

Ada was a shy single mother with a sick child. She desperately needed a job.

Four geographers and scientists (and a cat named Vic) were heading off on a grand adventure to the uninhabited Wrangel Island—fifty-five miles off the Northeast coast of Siberia. They needed a cook and seamstress.

Ada was hired. Her son Bennett was too ill for such a dangerous journey, so Ada made the heart-wrenching decision to leave him at an orphanage where he could get medical care. Her dream was to make enough money so they could be reunited.

The two year "grand adventure" quickly turned into a sad tale of survival.

The men had taken enough food to last six months—figuring they would hunt, trap, fish, and live off the land for the other eighteen months. Except none of them were hunters or trappers. At first, the men explored and studied the vegetation, rocks, and wildlife while Ada stayed behind. They kept journals, collected specimens, and created maps.

But then they ran into problems. Arctic storms raged, and they spent days huddled close to the fire. They worried about being attacked by the many polar bears roaming the area. Most of their food supplies had rotted.

They were slowly starving. It was time to abandon the expedition. One scientist was too ill to travel, so it was decided that Ada would stay and care for him while the others sought help. Ada collected seagull eggs for meals. She collected roots to eat, and found greens that tasted a little like watercress. She didn't know how to trap animals, but learned through trial and error. Ada walked for miles every day to check the traps—too often finding them empty.

She hated guns but taught herself to shoot—although she couldn't practice much for fear of running out of bullets. After a close encounter with a polar bear, Ada gathered wood and built a tall platform so she could keep an eye on them in all directions.

Despite her best efforts, the scientist died. Ada was now alone with only Vic, the cat, for company. A typewriter had been left behind, so she wrote about her days. It was almost like having a conversation with someone. Almost.

It would have been easy to give up, but Ada was determined to see her son again and just kept going, day after day. Then, two years later, Ada heard a loud rumbling noise. She grabbed her binoculars and stared through the fog. A ship! Rescued at last!

Ada's desire to see her son again gave her the courage and willpower to survive. Against all odds, she managed to do both!

BARBARA HILLARY

★ NORTH AND SOUTH POLE SENSATION ★

As a young girl being raised by a single mother in Harlem, Barbara loved reading exciting survival stories like *Robinson Crusoe* by Daniel Defoe. Maybe that's when she realized she had the soul of an adventurer!

Never one to shy away from hard work, Barbara accomplished many things during her lifetime—she earned her master's degree, worked in the healthcare field for over fifty-five years, and founded a nonprofit magazine.

But she wasn't done yet—far from it!

After winning a courageous battle with lung cancer, she decided to travel. But she wasn't interested in relaxing on a beach or being a typical tourist. Instead she wanted adventure! So she went dog-sledding. Then she photographed polar bears in Canada. Barbara fell in love with the beauty of the Arctic. And she set her sights on her next trip—going to the North Pole.

The North Pole isn't exactly an easy place to get to—you're dropped by helicopter onto an ice floe and then must ski to the Pole, pulling a sled with supplies.

Even though she had never skied before, Barbara was up to the challenge. She practiced by dragging a plastic sled across the beach—until the sand destroyed it. She also worked with a trainer to get into top physical shape.

The trip would be expensive—over $20,000—so she asked for donations and raised enough money to fund her expedition. Nothing was going to stop her. Not her age, her diminished lung capacity due to her cancer surgery, or her lack of funds. On April 23, 2007, this feisty, wisecracking, seventy-six-year-old dynamo set foot on the North Pole!

Barbara was the first African-American woman and possibly the oldest person to achieve this goal. She could have just sat back and relaxed while she reflected on her incredible feat. But that just wasn't in her nature. Instead, in 2011, she took another trip. This time she stood on the SOUTH Pole!

Still not ready to retire, Barbara has taken on new roles—as an inspirational speaker for cancer survivors and as an outspoken global-warming activist.

She shows no sign of slowing down—she's probably quietly planning her next adventure—although it will be hard to top her treks to both Poles. But if anyone is up to the challenge, it would be Barbara.

BEATRICE AYETTEY

★ UNCONVENTIONAL CAPTAIN ★

Beatrice grew up on the coast of Ghana—home to spectacular waterfalls, lakes, and sandy beaches. But she was not allowed to go near water—her mother considered it too dangerous. So she didn't learn to swim.

Unlike most girls in Ghana, who were expected to marry, stay home, and have children, Beatrice was in school planning on a career in medicine. But she was bored with her studies. Then an advertisement caught her eye—and changed her life!

It was an ad for Ghana Nautical College looking for applicants to be trained as cadets to man the country's fleet of merchant ships. Enrolling meant a complete change in her life's direction, a new field of study, the possibility of prejudice and resistance from male students and teachers, and once again, going against traditional gender roles. It also meant a life of adventure on the seas.

Adventure won. Surprisingly, she didn't encounter any hostility or discrimination while in class. That's because the men didn't take her seriously and expected her to drop out.

She didn't.

Beatrice graduated, became one of the first female cadets, and finally learned to swim. The work was physically and mentally demanding, but she was up to the task.

In 1990, Beatrice obtained her captain's license, a first for a woman in Ghana. It meant she would be responsible for the crew, the cargo, and the ship. Even though this tiny, barely five-foot-tall woman may be the only female on board, she still commands respect—and gets it. When she's at the helm of the 16,000-ton cargo ship *Keta Lagoon*, doing her job is the easy part. Dealing with long-held African superstitions can be harder. Many sailors believe that having a woman on board drives the fish away, or that she will anger and antagonize mermaids, resulting in devastating storms. By being successful in her duties, she is slowly putting long-standing superstitions to rest.

After twenty years at sea, Beatrice sought out new responsibilities. She went to work for the International Maritime Organization, which oversees shipping and helps prevent pollution of the world's oceans.

Her life may be unconventional, but Beatrice was a born sailor who was always ready and willing to accept and conquer the next challenge whether on land or at sea. She has steered a course, not only for her ship and her career, but for other women who aspire to a life of adventure, purpose, and excitement.

EMMA "GRANDMA" GATEWOOD

★ HIKER WITH HEART ★

Emma's life was anything but easy. She married at nineteen, but her husband soon became violent. To escape his cruelty, she often ran into the woods where she found peace. Getting a divorce was difficult for a woman back then—and she had eleven kids to think about. Finally, after thirty years of a disastrous marriage, she did something that was rare at that time: she obtained a divorce. Emma was now free to do whatever she wanted! She just didn't know what that was yet.

Emma had once seen breathtaking photographs accompanying an article in *National Geographic* magazine about the Appalachian Trail. It stated that a woman had never hiked the entire 2,050 miles. She decided to be the first!

Most hikers pack their supplies carefully, making sure they have the proper equipment. But Emma wasn't like other hikers. She had no special gear. In fact, she didn't even have a sleeping bag, compass, tent, or hiking boots. Emma *did* have a homemade denim bag, a raincoat, sneakers, a blanket, and a shower curtain. Her supplies barely weighed seventeen pounds.

In May 1955, at sixty-seven years old, off she went! The Appalachian Trail is not an easy walk—it meanders through fourteen states from Georgia to Maine. Emma encountered bears, rattlesnakes, two hurricanes, flooded streams, harsh brush, and huge boulders. She suffered lots of sprains, cuts, and bruises. She ate berries and plants along the way. But she mostly survived by what she called "trail magic"—other hikers sharing their food or giving her shelter when her shower curtain "tent" couldn't keep her dry and warm.

The hike was more difficult than she'd expected, and many times during her 146-day trek she wanted to quit. But she just kept going, overcoming all the obstacles she faced along the way.

In September, four months after she began, she reached the end of the trail in Maine. She celebrated being the first woman to do so by singing "America the Beautiful"!

But Emma wasn't done. Two years later, she hiked it AGAIN!

The publicity and media coverage she received during her hikes shined a much-needed spotlight on the Appalachian Trail and led to upgrades and restoration. It also captured the attention of a new generation of hikers who have attempted to follow in her footsteps.

Emma proved that it isn't where you come from, but where you're going that counts. And with hard work, dedication, and some worn-out sneakers, you can achieve success and inspire others to do the same.

DR. EUGENIE CLARK

★ SHARK LADY ★

Eugenie's life changed forever one Saturday afternoon when she was nine years old. Her mother had to go to work selling newspapers, and she didn't have a babysitter—so she dropped Eugenie off at the New York Aquarium. Eugenie's mother thought it would keep her busy and out of trouble. It did that—and so much more!

Eugenie marveled at all the different fish and sea creatures—she felt like she was in a magical world. And she went back, Saturday after Saturday. Soon their tiny apartment was filled with aquariums and fish tanks, and Eugenie became the youngest member of the Queens County Aquarium Society.

This wasn't a passing fad but a lifelong passion. She knew she wanted to become an ichthyologist—someone who studies fish and sharks. But her very first dive didn't go as planned. Deep below the surface, she realized something was wrong—she was running out of air! After being pulled up and into the boat, barely conscious, she saw that her air hose was leaking. It would have been easy to quit, but the lure of the ocean floor was too strong. Her hose was repaired by a crewmember and over the side she went!

Eugenie spent years diving and studying all types of fish and sea creatures around the world. But one species captured her attention the most—sharks. People perceived sharks as evil eating machines with little or no intelligence. Eugenie disagreed and made it her mission to prove otherwise.

To do so, she captured several lemon sharks and developed a test for them at her marine laboratory in Florida. Eugenie taught the sharks to swim into a target, which would ring a bell and release a bit of food as a reward. Then she made it harder—using different colored targets and different shapes. The sharks quickly adapted. Her groundbreaking research proved that sharks are highly intelligent and can be taught to do visual tasks.

She was up close and personal with sharks and never felt afraid. Once while she was diving, a forty-foot-long whale shark passed by, and she grabbed on for a great ride—letting go only when she saw how far away her boat was!

During her seventy-five-year career, Eugenie wrote, taught, and lectured about marine biology. She received numerous awards and honors, but her most important legacy was inspiring others to learn about, and fall in love with, her magical undersea world.

FANNY BULLOCK WORKMAN

 ★ COURAGEOUS CLIMBER ★

Fanny Bullock's childhood was one of wealth and privilege—fine schools, world travel, and fancy society parties. When she married Dr. William Hunter Workman in 1881, she could have stayed home and been a woman of leisure. But that lifestyle didn't suit Fanny. She wanted adventure and excitement!

During 1895, Fanny and William rode a bicycle built for two across Europe and Asia, through Spain to Morocco, over the Atlas Mountains, and into the Sahara Desert! William pedaled and steered from the front seat. They traveled light with only the most basic provisions, writing materials, a first aid kit, and a tire repair kit—which they used multiple times a day. For once, Fanny took a back seat to her husband, but only because she was armed with a revolver and a whip to discourage bandits they encountered along their way. She was a one-woman security team!

As they rode along, Fanny paid close attention to the local women and their living conditions, frequently snapping pictures with her Kodak camera. She kept careful notes on their travels, and these, along with her photos, were later published in eight travel books.

After bicycling about four thousand miles across the land from southern India to the Himalayas, they decided to travel up!

At that time, explorers had determined that the highest altitude climbers could reach—and survive—was 21,000 feet.

But they hadn't met Fanny!

In 1906, Fanny and William were the first Westerners to climb Pinnacle Peak—estimated at 23,000 feet—in the Nun Kun Range of the Himalayas. Fanny climbed very slowly in her long woolen skirts, alternating between boots and snowshoes. But her slow ascent was actually a benefit—it helped her to acclimate easily and avoid altitude sickness.

Besides traveling and trekking up mountains, Fanny's other passion was women's rights. She combined these two in 1912 when she posed for a photograph standing atop Siachen Glacier in the Himalayas holding up a newspaper with the headline *VOTES FOR WOMEN*.

In 1914, at the onset of World War I, Fanny hung up her snowshoes but continued to write about her travels and scientific observations. She was one of the first women to be admitted to the Royal Geographical Society and the first to lecture at the Sorbonne in Paris. She frequently hit the lecture circuit giving talks in English, French, or German, depending on where she was!

Not only was Fanny a courageous mountain climber, she was also proud to call herself a "New Woman," which meant she was equal to (and sometimes tougher than) any man!

FERMINIA SARRAS

★ COPPER QUEEN ★

Historians don't know exactly *how* Ferminia got from Nicaragua to Nevada, but they do know *why* she went there: gold fever!

It was during the time when men—and very few women—were willing to leave everything they knew behind in the hope of striking it rich.

All miners had to register in the County Courthouse before going prospecting. Ferminia signed her name "Ferminia Sarras, Spanish Lady." Two things about this new miner were shocking: first, she was a woman, and second, she bought herself pants! In those days, women wore only dresses.

Ferminia didn't care what anyone thought, and she bought herself the tools needed for prospecting: pickaxes, shovels, and boots. She added the most basic camping gear: a tin cup, a plate, and a tarp to use as a tent. Lugging her forty-pound pack, she set off into the hills to seek her fortune.

It wasn't easy. She endured extreme weather conditions—freezing temperatures in the winter, scorching heat in the summer. She hiked hundreds of miles in and out of canyons, through springs and up and over rocky hills, always on the lookout for snakes and coyotes. This went on for years, but she refused to give up.

In April 1883, Ferminia finally filed her first claim. That meant she had discovered a place worth mining and registered it as belonging to her. It would be the first of many!

Ferminia found bits of gold and silver, but she had a special knack for discovering copper. The more claims she staked, the more attention she received, until she became known as Nevada's "Copper Queen."

Once she had staked her claim, she would sell it to another miner or group of investors. Then she'd head back to the hills to find another one. Ferminia didn't trust banks, so she always insisted she be paid in gold. It was said she stashed the gold in her chicken coop because if anyone bothered the chickens, they'd squawk and raise a ruckus—making them an excellent burglar alarm!

Ferminia wasn't content to sit back and count her money—she loved to go to San Francisco and live it up. She'd buy fancy dinners and new clothes and stay in ritzy hotels. When her money ran out, she'd head back to the hills with her prospecting tools and search for another mine. When she met someone down on their luck, she didn't hesitate to invite them in and give them a hot meal. She was as generous as she was unconventional.

Ferminia lived a rich and adventurous life, not just because she was a miner, but because she had the courage to live life on her own terms.

IDA LEWIS

★ LIGHTHOUSE KEEPER AND LIFE SAVER ★

Ida Lewis's father was the Lime Rock lighthouse keeper in Rhode Island. The only way to get to the lighthouse was by boat. Ida loved the water and wanted to tag along. That meant she had to learn to row—and she did. Ida soon became as comfortable in a rowboat as she was on land! When she was fifteen, the family moved into the newly built lighthouse on Lime Rock. A few months later, her father became ill, and Ida took over his duties.

To keep ships from crashing into the rocks, the light had to burn all night, warning sailors of the danger. That meant Ida had to fill it with oil twice a night, trim the wick, and keep the glass clean and polished. That meant dropping out of school. But she still rowed her young siblings to and from school every day.

When she was sixteen, she made her first sea rescue. Four young men had capsized in the rough waters. Ida rowed out to them and hauled each one aboard her boat! It was a tremendous act of courage and strength for a young woman.

On March 25, 1869, two soldiers were caught in a storm. Their boat capsized and they were tossed into the freezing water. Despite the weather, Ida didn't hesitate. Without bothering to put on a coat, she sprinted to her boat and battled the crashing waves to ferry them to safety.

Ida didn't talk about her rescues—but the soldiers did! Soon, newspapers and magazines published stories about her courage and daring rescues. She was hailed as the "bravest woman in America." Congratulatory letters poured in from around the world. Thousands of people came to meet her, including one very famous visitor—President Ulysses S. Grant!

In her fifty-four years as a lighthouse keeper, she was credited with saving eighteen people. But the number is probably much higher—she never kept track.

Ida even inspired musicians—the "Ida Lewis Waltz" and "Rescue Polka Mazurka" were both written in her honor.

In 1881, the U.S. Coast Guard awarded Ida with the Gold Lifesaving Medal, and in 1907 she became the first woman to receive the American Cross of Honor.

In 1924, the name of the Lime Rock Lighthouse was officially changed to Ida Lewis Rock Lighthouse. It was an appropriate honor for this modest, brave, and steady-as-a-rock woman.

JEANNE BARET

★ SECRET SAILOR ★

Jeanne Baret grew up in poverty in France. But she still received an education—it just wasn't the kind one gets in a classroom. She received her education from nature. As a child she learned about the healing power of plants from her parents. She later became known as the "herb woman."

She eventually worked as a housekeeper for the naturalist Philibert Commerson. He shared her fascination with botany—the study of plants.

In 1766, the French government decided to send a ship on a scientific journey around the world. They needed a botanist to collect plant specimens along the way. Commerson was hired. Jeanne wanted to go too—but at that time it was illegal for a woman to sail on a French Navy ship.

Jeanne wasn't going to let that stop her from embarking on the trip of a lifetime, so she hatched a dangerous plan. She would disguise herself as a man, show up as the ship was about to set sail, and have Commerson "hire" her as his assistant.

Commerson agreed to help, and the plan worked! Jeanne wore baggy clothes and worked alongside the men. No matter how difficult or backbreaking the situation was, she continued on—earning her the nickname "beast of burden."

For two years, Jeanne dodged the suspicious crew, collected and catalogued over six thousand species of plants, and survived harsh living conditions in tight quarters. This was no vacation cruise. They endured foul weather, stormy seas, rats, and disease—on a diet of salted meat and hard biscuits.

One of their most famous discoveries was of a beautiful flowering plant. Jeanne gathered the seeds to bring back with her. Today, the plant is grown worldwide. But this amazing discovery doesn't bear Jeanne's name. It's known as the *bougainvillea*—after the French Admiral leading the expedition, Louis Antoine de Bougainville.

Nobody knows exactly how Jeanne's masquerade as a man was discovered—but it was. Even though she had broken the law, she'd been a valuable asset to the expedition, so she escaped imprisonment. But as punishment, Jeanne and Commerson were left on the island of Mauritius in the Indian Ocean while the ship returned to France. They continued to discover and study plants, amassing one of the world's greatest collections of specimens. Five years later, Commerson died, and Jeanne returned to France—becoming the first woman to circumnavigate the globe.

In 2012, Jeanne finally got the recognition as a botanist she deserved. A new South American flowering plant species—*Solanum baretiae*—was named in her honor. It's unique and interesting—just like Jeanne herself.

JOAN BAMFORD FLETCHER

★ REMARKABLE RESCUER ★

Joan grew up on a dairy farm in Canada. Her family was originally from England, so she attended boarding school there when she was old enough. She furthered her education in France and Belgium.

Joan eventually returned to Canada. And when World War II began, she wanted to do her part to help. She first trained as an ambulance driver for the Canadian Red Cross. It wasn't enough. Joan then joined the First Aid Nursing Yeomanry (FANY) and was sent to drive ambulances in Scotland for the exiled Polish army.

She still wanted to do more—and she got her chance, just as the war ended.

On September 2, 1945, the Japanese surrendered. But the plight of Dutch civilians held captive in the jungles of Sumatra did not end. They were living in horrible conditions. Disease was rampant. Food was scarce. They desperately needed help.

The entire area was in chaos. Japanese soldiers were trying to get back home. Allied soldiers had not arrived to protect and evacuate the prisoners. Indonesian rebels and other groups were still fighting for control.

Joan, now a twenty-three-year-old Canadian lieutenant, was sent to transfer the prisoners safely through the mountainous jungle to a port on the Indian Ocean—all two thousand of them. It would be an incredibly difficult, perhaps impossible, task.

She didn't hesitate.

The first thing she did was convince the Japanese army to loan her vehicles, armed soldiers, and a translator. They did—although they resented taking orders from a young woman. At least, at first.

Joan divided the prisoners into groups, and for six long weeks, she accompanied them on the hazardous twelve-hour journey to safety. Bridges had been blown up, so they had to use makeshift boats to get across rivers. Monsoon rains turned the already treacherous mountain roads into mud. The Indonesian rebels barricaded other roads while machine-gun toting Japanese guards kept them at bay. One day the rebels got too close, and Joan was hit by one of their trucks. After being stitched up and bandaged, she rejoined the convoy.

Despite the danger, Joan personally accompanied the prisoners on every single trip—all twenty trips. Although reluctant at first, the Japanese soldiers grew to respect and admire Joan's determination to complete her mission. One of the Japanese officers was so impressed by her courage that he presented her with his 300-year-old ancestral samurai sword.

In 1946, Joan was awarded the Order of the British Empire (M.B.E.) for her bravery and dedication to saving lives—an honor this hero so richly deserved.

JUNKO TABEI

★ MOUNTAINEERING MARVEL ★

As a young girl growing up in Japan, Junko was frail and sickly. She frequently battled pneumonia, fevers, and breathing problems. She never expected to do anything athletic. And besides, girls were expected to grow up, marry, and take care of their children and their home.

When Junko was ten years old, she went on a school field trip to climb Mount Asahi and Mount Chausu. That same year she climbed Mount Nasu with her fourth grade class, and a whole new world opened up to her. She was mesmerized by the breathtaking beauty of nature and the joy and peace she felt while climbing.

Junko continued to climb all through college, despite being ridiculed by male mountaineers who refused to climb with her. Junko would not give up her passion. So in 1969, she formed Japan's Ladies Climbing Club and spearheaded an all-female expedition to the Himalayas. Mountain climbing is expensive, and trips are usually funded by sponsors. But sponsors were scarce for female climbers. To keep costs down, the women made their own sleeping bags with goose feathers they bought from China, and waterproof bags and gloves from recycled materials.

What Junko loved most about mountain climbing is that it's not competitive—it's just you conquering the mountain at your own pace. And she was determined to do just that in 1975 when she set her sights on scaling Mount Everest. Near the top, disaster struck, and Junko was buried in an avalanche! She lost consciousness under several feet of snow and had to be dug out. Undaunted, she kept climbing. On May 16, 1975, she became the first woman to stand atop Mount Everest. Taking this amazing feat in stride, she remarked, "I can't understand why men make all the fuss about Everest. It's only a mountain."

And she was just getting started! Junko now had a new goal—to be the first woman to reach the highest point on all seven continents, known as the Seven Summits. And that's just what she did! After many years of climbing and persevering, she finally achieved her goal in 1992.

Junko's passion for the mountains she climbed grew and expanded into a new area—environmental conservation. She felt a great responsibility to care for the mountains that had given her so much joy. She regularly led "clean-up climbs" to pick up the trash left behind by the ever-increasing number of climbers in Japan and the Himalayas.

Junko passed her love of mountain climbing and the importance of caring for the environment to a new generation who are happily following in her footsteps.

LIBBY RIDDLES

★ MASTERFUL MUSHER ★

Libby Riddles spent much of her childhood outdoors—exploring the woods, eating berries, splashing in creeks, and climbing trees. When she was inside, she was enjoying her family's menagerie of animals, which included dogs, cats, fish, and birds.

Her dream was to live in the wilderness surrounded by animals. When she was just sixteen years old, Libby made that dream a reality. She graduated early from high school and moved to Alaska.

She built her own wood cabin, drank fresh water from a mountain stream, and chopped wood for her fireplace. In 1973, she was in the crowd watching the Open World Championship Sled Dog Race. She was captivated by its speed, power, and beauty. Libby had fallen in love at first sight—with dog mushing.

Training a sled dog team was much more difficult than training a pet. But Libby dedicated herself to the challenge. She worked closely with each individual dog to help it reach its potential. She believed in using her most important tool in the process—her common sense. And her training motto? The dogs come first.

In 1978, she entered her first race—and won!

Libby then set a goal—to race in the Iditarod, known as "the Last Great Race on Earth." It's a prestigious long-distance sled dog race and one of the most grueling. Held annually in Alaska, it tests the skill and endurance of the dogs and the musher as they race over one thousand miles in harsh weather conditions and rough terrain.

In 1980, Libby ran her first Iditarod. She came in eighteenth place. She tried again. And came in twentieth. Instead of giving up, Libby trained harder. In 1985, she was ready to try again. Sponsors weren't willing to put their money behind an unknown female musher, but the townspeople of Teller, Alaska, knew how dedicated, talented, and tough she was, and they donated their bingo money to help her out.

During the 1985 Iditarod, the weather was so treacherous that the race was shut down for days at a time. Libby battled blizzard conditions, temperatures of fifty degrees below zero, and long, dark nights with almost no visibility. After eighteen days, Libby crossed the finish line in first place—the first woman to win the Iditarod!

Libby continues to train her dogs and share her passion and love of sled dog racing through her books and lectures.

LILLIAN RIGGS

★ REMARKABLE RANCHER ★

L illian grew up on the ranch her parents had built as one of the first families to settle in Bonita Canyon in Arizona's Chiricahua Mountains. It was fondly referred to as "Faraway Ranch" because it WAS far away from everything!

As a young girl she helped with all aspects of cattle ranching—branding, roping, and herding. Her circumstances taught her to be self-sufficient and adaptable. If something was broken, you fixed it. If a cow was sick, you nursed it back to health. If you were hungry, you picked vegetables from the garden. That lesson stuck with Lillian throughout her life.

She left home to further her education and spent several years teaching. Faraway Ranch went through some hard times after a severe drought, so the family opened it up to visitors wanting to experience life on a working ranch. Lillian returned to help with both enterprises—raising cattle and operating a "dude ranch," a vacation destination where people learned how a cattle ranch was run by helping out.

One day while Lillian was hiking with her husband, Ed, they discovered several stunning rock formations—an area that is now known as the Wonderland of Rocks. Lillian and Ed built hiking trails so more people could enjoy them, which also helped bring in more guests to the dude ranch. The area eventually became part of the Chiricahua National Monument.

In 1942, Lillian went blind. Then in 1950, more tragedy struck. Lillian's mother and Ed both died. Everyone expected her to sell the ranch—it would be impossible for her to remain in charge. Or so they thought.

Lillian had no intention of leaving. Just as she had done as a child, she adapted. She still covered her ranch on horseback—one hand on her reins, the other holding a rope attached to her riding companion's saddle.

She continued to be a hands-on cattle rancher—literally! As the cattle went through the chute, she felt their teeth and shanks to decide which ones to sell and which ones to keep. It was said she could recognize each cow by touch!

To check the condition of the pasture, she knelt on the ground and touched the grass to determine if it was fresh and tall enough for the cattle to graze upon.

Lillian remained in charge of Faraway Ranch into her eighties, never letting her blindness slow her down. She fully embodied the rough-and-tumble, can-do spirit of the American West!

MARGARET BOURKE–WHITE

★ FEARLESS PHOTOGRAPHER ★

Margaret didn't like to stay in one place for very long. She attended six different colleges before graduating from Cornell in 1927. She became interested in photography and took pictures of the campus buildings—and sold them for extra money.

After graduating, she developed a reputation for having a keen eye for architectural and industrial photography. Margaret would go anywhere to get the perfect shot! She once perched on a stone gargoyle outside her studio, sixty-one stories high, to get a bird's-eye view of New York City.

She combined her love of photography with her passion for travel. Wearing snowshoes, she braved freezing temperatures to capture the rugged beauty of logging camps. She also hiked down into South African mines and sat in the open door of a helicopter—anything to capture just the right shot.

In 1930, in a field dominated by men, she became a photographer for *Fortune* magazine.

She was sent on an assignment and became the first Western photographer allowed in Russia. She captured images of not only the factories, but the workers as well. Margaret realized she wanted to share their stories with the world so her focus shifted to people rather than buildings. She captured many emotions with her lens, from joy to despair.

In 1934, *Fortune* sent her to document the Dust Bowl, a huge swath of drought-stricken land stretching across the southwestern states. Margaret took photos of the devastated farmlands from an airplane but also captured the pain and emotion on the faces of those affected.

In 1941, during World War II, Margaret was sent to Moscow. She risked her life to photograph twenty-two German bombing attacks from atop the U.S. embassy. She became an Air Force photographer, and despite the danger, she was placed on a troop ship headed to North Africa. The ship was torpedoed by a German submarine! She managed to board a lifeboat and was rescued the next day.

Undaunted by her brush with death, she convinced the Air Force to let her fly with the crew of a B-17 bomber. She spent two weeks with them, and her photos appeared in *Life* magazine.

Margaret also traveled with General Patton's troops and took haunting photos of the Nazi concentration camps. Her images brought the horrors of war to the public in ways they'd never seen before.

Throughout her career, Margaret fearlessly risked her life to accurately photograph and document events around the world. With her keen eye, she captured some of humankind's greatest moments and achievements and also some of the most dire and tragic situations. But one thing always shone through her work—the incredible power of the human spirit.

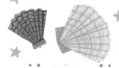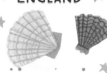

MARY ANNING

★ FOSSIL FINDER AND DINOSAUR DISCOVERER ★

Mary spent her whole life in the seaside town of Lyme Regis in Dorset, England. As a child she loved to hunt for interesting rocks, seashells, and fossils with her father and brother. They then sold their discoveries to tourists as vacation souvenirs.

When Mary was eleven years old, her father died, leaving the family in a tough situation. To help out, Mary left school and continued her dangerous hobby of collecting trinkets to sell. She spent her days hiking, climbing, and dodging rocks as they tumbled down the crumbling cliffs. She nimbly avoided tides and crashing waves along the beach. Mary continued to sell fossils, rocks, and seashells—so many that the tongue twister "She sells seashells by the seashore" was written about her!

She soon made her most important discovery. After a storm, she spotted something interesting. Mary used her hammer and chiseled out something big. And strange.

It was a skeleton of a creature nobody had ever seen before! It had the head of a crocodile, the body of a lizard, flippers, and a shark's tail.

Mary had discovered an *ichthyosaurus*, which is Latin for "fish lizard." The word "dinosaur" didn't even exist at that time. She hired workmen to carry it to her home. A wealthy businessman bought it and placed it on display in a museum.

Her find shook up the scientific world in many ways. Before this, nobody had realized a species could become extinct. The skeleton was two hundred million years old, which shattered the previously held belief that the earth was only six thousand years old. And paleontology, an entirely new field of study, was born. Scientists were forced to accept the fact that the natural world changed over time.

Mary continued to scour the cliffs for fossils and made even more astonishing discoveries! She found an almost complete *plesiosaur* or "near lizard." She also found a fossil that was the missing link between stingrays and sharks. And some of the interesting stones that she collected turned out not to be stones at all! They were actually bezoars—essentially, mineral-laden hairballs formerly believed to have medicinal properties.

Many of Mary's fossils have since been displayed in museums and have been written about in books and journals by geologists and scientists. But at that time, Mary didn't receive any credit. And not because it wasn't deserved—but because she was a woman.

Just as the natural world changes over time, however, so has the attitude about women scientists—thanks in part to the daring discoveries of Mary Anning!

MINA HUBBARD

★ EXTRAORDINARY EXPLORER ★

Mina was born on an apple farm in Ontario, Canada, but unlike some of the other girls her age, she wasn't content to stay there. She wanted a career. Mina completed her nurse's training and was soon taking care of an interesting patient. Leonidas Hubbard was a journalist suffering from typhoid fever. He became much more than her patient—the two fell in love and got married.

As an assistant editor for *Outing* magazine, Leonidas frequently went on wilderness camping trips—and Mina occasionally accompanied him. In 1903, he set out on a bold expedition without Mina to map the wild and virtually unexplored Labrador region of eastern Canada. Mina waited patiently for his return. Unfortunately, Leonidas died on the journey, leaving Mina grief-stricken.

Leonidas's travel partner, Dillon Wallace, barely survived the trip.

Mina encouraged Dillon to write a book about the expedition. She expected him to hail her husband as a talented explorer and hero. He did not. Instead, he claimed Leonidas was incompetent and responsible for his own death.

Now, besides sorrow, Mina was filled with another emotion—anger. She decided to retrace her husband's steps and complete his journey, hoping to restore his reputation.

On June 27, 1905, Mina and four men who would help carry supplies and paddle the canoes set out on the 576-mile trip through the unmapped area of Labrador to Ungava Bay. But Dillon Wallace was also ready to try again. The two set out on the same day—the race was on!

Mina followed her late husband's route and used a sextant to carefully navigate their course. The group encountered miles of rapids and rough waters. Occasionally they carried the canoes and supplies over rough terrain to the next body of water. Mice got into their food supplies. Flies, insects, and mosquitos were a constant nuisance.

No matter how difficult the journey got, Mina refused to turn back.

All along the journey, she collected plant specimens, took photos, and carefully drew accurate maps of the area. They ate berries, baked biscuits over the open fire, caught fish, and made jerky out of caribou. Although the meat helped them survive, Mina didn't like killing such beautiful animals.

She also met and took photos of both the Naskaupi and Montagnais tribes, taking careful notes of their clothing, homes, diet, and customs.

On August 27, they reached their destination, six weeks before her rival, Dillon Wallace!

Mina finished what her husband had started—and fulfilled both of their dreams.

ROSALY LOPES

★ DARING DISCOVERER ★

For as long as she can remember, Rosaly has been fascinated by science. As a young girl, when asked what she wanted to be when she grew up, she immediately answered—an astronaut! She loved gazing up into the night sky dreaming of a future job at NASA.

In 1978, she was a student at the University of London, still on the career track she'd chosen as a child. Then something happened that threw her off course. Mount Etna erupted off the coast of Sicily! Rosaly's attention suddenly shifted from outer space to the earth. Studying volcanoes sounded more exciting than staring at distant stars and planets through a telescope.

A year later, Rosaly was doing graduate school fieldwork in Sicily when Mount Etna erupted again a mile away! When she saw hot, flowing lava for the first time, she described it as being alive and breathing—and she fell in love with its awesome power and otherworldly beauty. While she respected the danger, she was mesmerized and wanted to see more volcanoes up close and personal. Once she even cooked on a lava flow!

In 1981, Mount Etna erupted again and Rosaly and other scientists rushed to Sicily. Travel delays meant they arrived after the volcano had quieted. Rosaly was disappointed but still wanted a closer look. She quickly discovered it hadn't cooled yet and could erupt again at any second. And it did! Rosaly dodged exploding lava bombs and fiery rocks while sprinting to safety.

In 1989, Rosaly fulfilled her dream of working at NASA in its Jet Propulsion Laboratory. It allowed her to combine her two passions—astronomy and volcanoes. She studied volcanoes on moons, and applied that knowledge to better understand volcanic eruptions on Earth.

There are many different types of volcanoes, and each one is unique—information she wanted to share with others. She did just that in her book *The Volcano Adventure Guide*—the first travel guide ever written for adventurers wanting a closer look.

In 1991, she was a member of the Galileo Flight Project, where she studied Jupiter's volcanic moon Io. During that time, she discovered seventy-one active volcanoes—more than any other person in the world—landing her in the Guinness Book of World Records.

Rosaly has written books and hundreds of articles on volcanoes, both here on Earth and elsewhere in the solar system. Her passion for science and the desire to educate others has never wavered. This very busy volcanologist has been featured in over twenty science documentaries and has received many awards and accolades in her field.

SYLVIA EARLE

★ UNDERWATER WANDERER ★

You could describe Sylvia Earle as a child in one word—CURIOUS! She was born in New Jersey and loved exploring the nearby woods and ponds. She studied everything from weeds to rocks. And she wrote about what she observed in notebooks. Her mother called these her "investigations." When she was twelve, her family moved to Florida, and she had something new to explore in her backyard—the Gulf of Mexico!

Sylvia became one of the first female oceanographers. She loved everything about oceans—the creatures, the reefs, and especially the plants—cataloging over twenty thousand plant specimens during her career.

Sylvia enjoyed scuba diving but wanted to know what it was like to actually live underwater. In 1970, with four other women, she spent two weeks in the deep-sea station *Tektite II*. It was fifty feet below the water's surface off the Virgin Islands. This allowed her to swim for hours—both day and night—without having to surface. While she was there, she discovered twenty-six new underwater plants.

After the women surfaced, the media took notice, and the aquanauts were given a ticker-tape parade and a reception at the White House. This publicity gave her a platform from which she could educate people on ocean conservation and the devastation of pollution.

In 1979, she made a record-setting dive of 1,250 feet. She wore an atmospheric diving suit called a JIM suit, which looked like an astronaut's pressurized suit. She went deeper than anyone else ever had. Sylvia explored for two and a half hours, untethered and alone. The tiniest tear in her suit would have crushed her immediately due to the immense underwater pressure—yet she was never afraid while diving. She even planted an American flag while she was down there!

Diving can be dangerous. Sylvia was once stung by a poisonous lionfish, and another time had to kick a shark to keep from being bit. And swimming too close to humpback whales caused her body to vibrate so hard it hurt—but it was worth it to hear them "sing."

She spent over seven thousand hours underwater, earning her the nicknames "Her Deepness" and the "Sturgeon General." She was named "Hero of the Planet" by *Time* magazine and received over a hundred national and international honors and awards, including being named Conservationist of the Year in 1998.

Sylvia founded the nonprofit Mission Blue to fund ocean exploration and protect the oceans—a cause she believes in wholeheartedly.

❧ YNES MEXIA ❧

★ BRAVE BOTANIST ★

When Ynes was a young child, life was carefree and fun. She spent more time riding horses and exploring outdoors than she did in school. And she liked it that way!

Then things changed. Her parents divorced, and life got tough. At first, she lived with her mother in Texas. Later, she lived with her father in Mexico City. Ynes was unhappy and restless. She married and divorced—twice. Finally, when she was fifty-five years old, she moved to San Francisco for a fresh start. Her doctor encouraged her to exercise, so she started hiking. It changed her life. Her love of the outdoors blossomed into a new passion: botany, the study of plant life. She no longer felt she was wandering through life—now she had a purpose!

Ynes studied botany at the University of California in Berkeley, not caring that she was the oldest student in class. But reading about plants wasn't enough. She wanted to go out and *find* plants—ones that nobody had ever seen before!

It wasn't going to be easy. Women weren't taken seriously as plant collectors—expeditions were considered too difficult and physically demanding. And an inexperienced middle-aged woman trekking through forests and jungles? No way!

Ynes didn't care what anyone said, and she boarded a steamship to Mexico. She spent the next seven months exploring and collecting plants. Much of the time she worked alone. Other times she hired guides who took her to remote areas both on horseback and on foot. She took photographs of trees, plants, shrubs, and moss. Then she dried the specimens, packed them up, and shipped them back to the States. No matter what challenges she faced—mosquitoes, ticks, snakes, spiders, storms, heat, rugged terrain, primitive camping—she just kept going. Only after she tumbled off a cliff and broke several ribs did she take a break!

Interesting plants were everywhere—and that's where Ynes went. For twelve years, she explored dry highlands, low wetlands, mountains, and rain forests in Mexico, Brazil, Peru, Argentina, Chile, Ecuador, and Alaska.

Ynes's dream of finding a new plant species came true—several times! Many plants have been named in her honor. Because of her hard work and determination, she's considered to be one of the most important and skilled botanists of the twentieth century. She collected over 150,000 specimens—many of which are still being studied today.

Ynes proved that you are never too old to follow your passion—wherever it may lead.

Rebels

ALIA MUHAMMAD BAKER

★ LIONHEARTED LIBRARIAN ★

Alia Muhammad Baker loves books! She was proud to be the chief librarian in the Al Basrah Central Library in Basra, Iraq. The collection had books in many languages. There were new books and old books. *Really* old books. One was a seven-hundred-year-old biography of Muhammad!

The library was much more than bookshelves—it was also a community center. People gathered there every afternoon to discuss a wide variety of subjects.

In 2003, Iraq was at war. American and British forces were planning to oust Iraq's dictator, Saddam Hussein, from power. Troops were coming closer to Basra, and people were worried about their town, their homes, and their lives.

Alia was also worried about the library and its priceless books.

First, she went to the government and asked for the books to be moved to safety.

Her request was denied.

Even worse, government officials moved into the library and situated an anti-aircraft gun on its roof.

Would the library now become a target?

Alia began taking books out of the library and to her home for safekeeping. Before long, her house was crammed full of books—but there were still so many at the library.

The war was inching closer. Explosions and gunshots pierced the air. Fire and devastation were all around. Buildings were looted—including the library. The furniture, carpets, and light fixtures were gone. But the books remained!

Alia knew she had to act quickly. She talked to Anis Muhammad, who owned the Hamdan, a popular restaurant next to the library. They enlisted family members, friends, neighbors—anyone willing to help. They bundled priceless books in the library curtains and formed a book-moving brigade. They passed them over a seven-foot wall into the restaurant. Book by book, hour after hour. Not everyone who volunteered could read or write, yet they knew the books were precious.

Days later, disaster struck. Between the gunfire and bombs, the library caught fire and was destroyed. But thanks to Alia and her helpers, 70 percent of the collection had been rescued—thirty thousand books were stacked safely in the restaurant and at her home!

Alia wasn't finished. She hired a truck and moved the books to the homes of friends, family members, neighbors, and shopkeepers.

The library was rebuilt in 2004, and the books were returned. Before she could return as the librarian, Alia suffered a stroke. But that was not going to stop her! After she recovered, she returned as the chief librarian of the library that she loved—and had saved.

ANNETTE KELLERMAN

 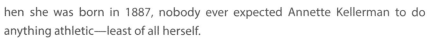

★ MERMAID QUEEN ★

When she was born in 1887, nobody ever expected Annette Kellerman to do anything athletic—least of all herself.

Due to illness, she had weak, crooked legs and wore heavy braces for support. This caused her to walk slowly and stiffly. To avoid being teased, she kept to herself.

When she was six, her doctor recommended routine exercise to strengthen her legs. So Annette took swimming lessons. And hated them! But the more she practiced, the better she got. Her legs grew stronger, and soon she no longer needed braces.

By fifteen, she was a talented swimmer and diver and started competing—and winning! Her passion led her to a unique job. Dressed in a mermaid costume, Annette did two shows a day swimming among fish at the Exhibition Aquarium in the largest glass tank in the world.

She was a star swimmer in Australia but wanted to further her career, so she moved to London. Sadly, no one was interested in a mermaid show. But she'd had a taste of fame and wanted more. What could she do to get attention? Her talent was swimming…so she swam thirteen miles down the Thames River—something no man had ever done! People were astonished, and she became front-page news. The British media called her the "Australian Mermaid."

Annette then decided to take her skills to America. She performed water ballets in vaudeville shows wearing elaborate costumes. Her career was on the rise. But then something awful happened.

In 1907, she was arrested. Had she robbed a bank? Blackmailed someone? Committed murder? No. She had worn a one-piece bathing suit to Revere Beach in Massachusetts. It covered her from her neck to her ankles—but it exposed her bare arms.

Scandalous! Shocking! And illegal.

It was similar to what she'd worn in Australia and London, but in the States, women were not encouraged to swim. They would daintily dip their toes in the water—dressed in swimming suits with stockings, skirts, sleeves, bonnets and rows of ruffles.

During her court trial, Annette told the judge, "I can't swim wearing more clothes than you would hang on a clothesline."

She won. And she started a line of women's bathing suits called "Kellermans." They did not have stockings or sleeves!

Annette wrote swimming manuals, and books about beauty, health, and exercise. She was also a silent film star in underwater spectaculars with stunts like diving into a pool of live crocodiles!

She believed her greatest achievement wasn't holding ALL the women's swimming records in 1905, or the books she wrote—it was creating a suit so women could freely enjoy swimming as much as she did.

ANNIE "LONDONDERRY" COHEN KOPCHOVSKY

★ BODACIOUS BICYCLIST ★

Annie was born in Latvia and immigrated to Boston as a child. At twenty-three, she was a restless wife and mother. She heard that two wealthy businessmen had made a wager—if a woman rode a bike around the world in fifteen months, they'd pay her $10,000. Nobody knows exactly who made the wager, or if it actually happened, but either way, Annie was ready to go!

After just a few bicycling lessons, Annie packed one change of clothes and a pearl-handled revolver in case she ran into bandits along the way. Dressed in heavy long skirts, a high-necked collared shirt and a flat hat, she mounted a forty-two-pound Columbia bicycle. The Londonderry Lithia Springs Water Company gave her a sign to hang on her bike and $100 for advertising their product during her trip. She also agreed to go by the name "Annie Londonderry," which helped promote both of them along the way.

On June 25, 1894, Annie waved to a large crowd in front of Boston's statehouse and pedaled away on her round-the-world journey.

Riding the heavy bike was harder than she expected. In Chicago, the Sterling Bicycle Company gave her a much lighter men's bike in exchange for her carrying advertisements and banners for their company. Annie changed more than her bike—she changed her attitude toward women's fashions. Pedaling in long skirts was hot and difficult, so she switched to bloomers—baggy pants gathered at the knee which were considered scandalous at the time. Later she wore men's pants and a vest. Some people were shocked. Others were intrigued. Annie encouraged women along the way to take up bicycling *and* her new manner of dressing. Many women did both!

Annie had planned on riding across the country to the West Coast, but she realized that would be impossible during the winter. She changed direction and headed to New York. Then she boarded a steamship to France, biked, and boarded another ship to Egypt. She was an enthusiastic and spellbinding storyteller and captivated audiences who paid to hear of her adventures. She didn't hesitate to "embellish" her stories to make them more exciting and suspenseful. Annie also earned money along the way by selling autographed photographs of herself and carrying advertising signs, banners, flags, and posters for all types of products—like what race car drivers do today with their cars!

Fifteen months to the day, Annie returned home triumphant. The *New York World* proclaimed it to be "the most extraordinary journey ever taken by a woman." She had proved to be an excellent athlete, self-promoter, human advertisement, and fashion icon.

Annie's journey was so much more than a long bicycle ride—it helped change attitudes about fashion and about women and their roles in society.

BELLE BOYD

★ SLY SPY ★

When Belle Boyd grew up in the South, girls were supposed to be ladylike, demure, and quiet. But she was none of those things!

After she was told she couldn't join her parents and their guests at dinner because she was a child, Belle rode her horse into the dining room in protest.

Belle attended a fancy boarding school to learn how to be a well-rounded young lady. Instead of taming her rebellious ways, she became even more mischievous, even carving her name into a window.

The Civil War broke out when she was in her teens. She was fiercely loyal to the South and wanted to do her part to help the Confederacy. Belle attended parties and flirted with the Union soldiers—and uncovered information about their upcoming missions. She then sent messages to the Confederate soldiers in a variety of clever ways. Belle hid notes in her hair, sewed them into the soles of her shoes, and stuffed them inside loaves of bread.

When she was seventeen, a message she'd sent was confiscated. It was written in her own handwriting, and she'd signed her name. Belle was arrested for being a spy. It could mean years in prison—or possibly execution. But she charmed the Union soldiers and was released because they didn't believe a young girl posed a threat.

They were wrong.

Belle became bolder. She attended social gatherings with Union soldiers. They would remove their weapons and leave them in a room before entering the party. Belle would hide their guns and swords under her hoop skirt and later give them to Confederate soldiers.

In May 1862, Belle learned of an important meeting being held in a nearby hotel. She eavesdropped through a knothole in the wood. She then rode her horse fifteen miles in the middle of the night to warn General Thomas "Stonewall" Jackson of the plans she'd heard. The more daring she became, the more people talked about her exploits. Newspaper articles were written about the "Siren of the Shenandoah." Belle was arrested and released several times—usually after charming her guards.

After the war, Belle realized she had been wrong to support the Confederacy. Once she was mature enough to understand the consequences of her actions, she felt the need to make up for her work as a spy. So she used her notoriety to speak out against the war and slavery. She traveled the country lecturing and encouraging unity between the North and the South. Belle's cleverness was what made her so successful as a spy. But she also proved that a woman can be bold and daring by admitting when she's wrong.

BESSIE STRINGFIELD

★ "MOTORCYCLE QUEEN OF MIAMI" ★

Bessie was born in Jamaica. She and her family moved to Boston when she was a young girl. When Bessie was only five years old, her parents died. An Irish woman adopted and raised her.

On her sixteenth birthday, Bessie asked for just one thing. Even though women at that time didn't ride motorcycles, that was what she wanted. And she got one! She quickly taught herself to ride and became quite skilled.

At nineteen, she started taking "penny tours" across the country. Bessie would flip a penny onto a map, and that's where she'd go! This allowed her to visit all forty-eight lower states during eight cross-country trips. Not everyone was supportive of a woman traveling alone on a motorcycle. Bessie also frequently encountered racial prejudice, but she didn't let that stop her from doing what she loved. If she was refused a room at a hotel, Bessie would just sleep on her motorcycle outside a gas station. She'd put her jacket on the handlebars for a pillow and stretch out along the seat.

To earn money during her trips, she would perform motorcycle stunts at carnivals and fairs. Her signature move was riding her motorcycle while standing on the seat. Bessie once entered a motorcycle race disguised as a man. She won! But when she took off her helmet and revealed that she was a woman, they refused to award her the prize money.

During World War II, Bessie worked as a civilian courier for the U.S. Army. She would deliver documents and important papers on her motorcycle from base to base across the United States.

When she settled in Miami, she again faced prejudice and resentment. Once Bessie was run off the road by a man in a pickup truck. She was also pulled over and harassed by local policemen who didn't believe a woman—especially a black woman—should be riding a motorcycle. Bessie asked the police captain to meet her in a nearby park. She then proved what a talented rider she was—and the harassment stopped.

Bessie founded the Iron Horse Motorcycle Club and encouraged other women to learn to ride. In 2002, she was inducted into the Motorcycle Hall of Fame. The AMA (American Motorcycle Association) created the Bessie Stringfield award in her honor. The award is given to outstanding women motorcyclists. She owned twenty-eight motorcycles during her lifetime and rode right up to her death at eighty-two, earning her the much-deserved nickname "the Motorcycle Queen of Miami."

ELLA HATTAN

★ QUEEN OF THE SWORD ★

Ella's father was a tailor who died in the Civil War. Her mother was Spanish and taught her to fence when she was just a child. When Ella was about eighteen years old, she enrolled in the School of Arms to be trained by the famous swordsman Colonel Monstery. He didn't take it easy on her just because she was a woman, and soon she had mastered broadswords, foils, daggers, lances, and bayonets. If it had a blade, Ella knew how to use it!

Fencing and sword fighting were popular spectator sports in the 1880s. But dueling on solid ground wasn't exciting enough—so the sport evolved into equestrian fencing—sword fighting on horseback. Opponents would mount their horses, race towards each other, and try to knock each other off—looking like medieval knights in a jousting contest.

Ella was also an actress, and when she combined her love of performing with her skill with blades, she became a popular attraction. She traveled the country billed as "The World-Renowned Jaguarina, the Ideal Amazon of the Age."

In April 1896, she faced U.S. military veteran Sergeant Charles Walsh in front of four thousand spectators. She mounted her horse *Muchacho* and galloped across the field toward him. Without hesitation, she knocked him off his horse. She had struck him so hard her sword had bent backwards! Instead of dusting himself off, remounting, and continuing the match, he sprinted off the field.

Ella was declared the winner.

She kept training and won match after match after match. Ella wasn't just good with a sword—she was almost *too* good. By 1897, she had beaten over sixty men in contests—both on foot and on horseback. She was having trouble finding new opponents—nobody wanted to compete with the "Queen of the Sword"!

Ella placed advertisements in newspapers offering $5,000 to anyone who could beat her. Nobody took her up on her offer.

With no willing opponents, she began teaching fencing to other women. She also went back on stage, appearing in small theaters across the country. Ella even trained to become a matador but quickly realized that wasn't going to work out—she would much rather give the bull hay than hurt him.

Ella was the greatest swordswoman of the nineteenth century—excelling in a sport usually dominated by men. This incredible athlete carved a wide path for other women to follow in her footsteps.

IRENA SENDLER

★ HEROINE OF THE HOLOCAUST ★

When Irena was in high school she realized that not everyone was treated equally. She and her Catholic friends were separated from the Jewish students and told not to sit with them. She refused to obey and was suspended. Her sense of fairness and courage to stand up for her beliefs would last a lifetime.

Irena was working for the Social Welfare Department in Warsaw when World War II broke out. In 1940, over 500,000 Jews were imprisoned by the Nazis in the Warsaw Ghetto, which was surrounded by tall brick walls and armed guards. Living conditions were horrible. There wasn't enough food, fresh water, or medicine.

A secret organization—code name: Zegota—formed to help the imprisoned Jewish families. Irena was one of the first to join.

She was permitted to enter the ghetto to look for signs of disease, but she was doing something else—smuggling out children.

Irena came up with clever ways to sneak the children out—sometimes right in front of the guards. She carried babies out in packages, suitcases, and potato sacks. She hid them under the floorboards of the ambulance or in the garbage truck—buried beneath trash. Older children would sneak into the back door of a church, change clothes, and walk out the front door. They were carefully coached to answer questions by the guards. None of them were caught.

The children would be given forged documents and sent to live with foster families or relatives. Irena carefully wrote down each child's true name—and their new identity—on a slip of paper. She placed the names into a jar and buried it underneath an apple tree. She hoped that someday the children would be reunited with their families.

Irena risked her life smuggling children to safety almost daily for eighteen months. But on October 20, 1943, she was arrested. For three months, she was imprisoned and tortured, but she refused to give up the names of the children or her coworkers. She was saved from execution when members of the Zegota bribed her guards and they released her.

She returned to Warsaw using a false name and continued rescuing children. In 1945, when the war ended, Irena dug up the jar and gave the children's names—all 2,500 of them—to the Jewish National Committee.

Irena always wished she could have done even more. She never saw herself as a hero—but that's exactly what a true hero would say.

JOHANNA JULY

★ HORSE WHISPERER ★

As a child living in northern Mexico, Johanna didn't do what girls were "supposed" to do at that time. She didn't cook, sew, or clean. Instead, she tagged along with her father and brother, hunting and fishing right alongside them. They lived on a settlement with other Black Seminoles—descendants of escaped slaves and Seminole Indians. Johanna loved being outside—but she hated wearing shoes and spent most of her life barefoot!

In 1871, the family moved to Fort Duncan, Texas. Her job was to take care of the horses, making sure they always had fresh water and hay, which meant cutting and hauling it home herself. Horse thieves were a constant threat. Once she spied some thieves in the distance, and she had to jump on her horse and gallop wildly to safety, the herd following along behind her.

She was also expected to herd the family's goats and cattle. It was a lot to handle for a young girl, but she was up to the task.

When Johanna's father died, she took over his job too—taming wild horses. This was a dangerous task even for a strong man, but this petite young girl developed her own unique method for wrangling wild mustangs.

Dressed in colorful homemade dresses, with lots of necklaces and long dangly earrings, she stood out among the other ranch hands and cowboys. But they soon learned not to underestimate her skills.

Johanna didn't like using a saddle, but preferred to ride bareback. Instead of leather reins, she used an old rope looped over her horse's nose. She would ride her tame horse to circle a herd of wild horses, then she'd choose one horse from the herd and drive it into the Rio Grande River. Then she'd slip off her horse, wade into the river, and swim up to the wild mustang. Walking against the current would wear the wild horse out, and Johanna would be able to gently climb onto its back and talk softly to soothe the horse. Eventually, the horse would relax, and she would be able to coax it back onto land. It was as if she and the horse had an unspoken bond, and a mutual admiration for one another.

Johanna soon became known as the *dormadora*, or the breaker of horses. Not only did she tame horses for her family, but she also worked for the U.S. Army and nearby ranchers who appreciated her remarkable skill and technique.

Johanna spent her entire life around her beloved horses—and that's just the way she liked it.

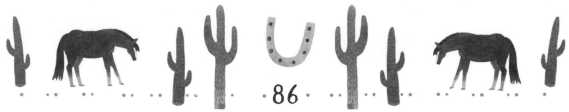

KATE WARNE

★ DARING DETECTIVE ★

When Kate was twenty-three years old, there were no female police officers. No female detectives. Women didn't even have the right to vote. So when she walked into the Pinkerton Detective Agency and asked for a job, the odds were against her. Yet somehow, she was hired as the first female detective in America!

Kate insisted she could ferret out information that a man couldn't and that no one would ever guess a woman was a detective. Against his brother's wishes, Allan Pinkerton was open-minded enough to give her a try. In 1858, she was put to the test when she worked undercover in a major embezzlement case. Kate made friends with the suspect's wife and was able to get her to spill her secrets! With the information Kate received, the man was arrested, convicted, and sent to prison.

She was also a master of disguise. Sometimes she gathered information dressed as a fortune teller, other times as a wealthy widow. Kate often used fake names and accents—whatever the job required.

In 1861, Kate had her biggest and most important case. The Pinkerton detectives were hearing disturbing rumblings from a group of secessionists—southerners who wanted to assassinate President Abraham Lincoln before he could free the slaves. The detectives needed specific details if they were going to thwart the diabolical plot. They needed someone brave and clever to get close enough to infiltrate their group. They needed Kate.

She went undercover dressed as a southern belle—with an accent sweet as molasses. Kate put a black and white ribbon in her hatband—a secret signal that she was a secessionist—and joined the festivities and meetings at the Barnum Hotel. Kate was able to uncover more details of the assassination plot. The attempt on Lincoln's life would take place during his journey to Washington, D.C. Part of his route required him to change trains in Baltimore. The assassination was to take place while he was on a mile-long buggy ride between stations.

The detectives needed a plan to keep Lincoln safe. And Kate had one. She reserved four berths on the D.C.-bound train for her ailing brother and family members. When Lincoln's train arrived in Baltimore, Kate accompanied a weak, limping man in a shawl to the next train. Nobody realized it was Lincoln in a disguise. He made it safely back to Washington, D.C.

After Kate proved that women were just as capable as, and in some situations, more valuable than their male counterparts, Pinkerton hired more women as detectives. Kate was put in charge of training an all-female investigative staff—forging the way for countless other women to have successful careers in law enforcement.

KEIKO FUKUDA

★ AMAZING MARTIAL ARTIST ★

When Keiko was a young girl growing up in Japan, she may not have realized how revered or important her grandfather was in the area of martial arts. Fukuda Hachinosuke had been a samurai, a jujitsu master, and a teacher. One of his students, Jigoro Kano, was the founder of judo.

As a child, Keiko followed tradition and learned the art of flower arranging, calligraphy, and the precise and intricate details of tea ceremonies.

But one day she went with her mother and watched a judo training session.

Keiko was hooked!

In judo, you use your opponent's strength, weight, and momentum against them. That was perfect for Keiko. She had a lot of determination and dedication, but at just under five feet tall, her tiny size would be a hindrance in most physical sports.

At first, Keiko trained alone, mirroring the moves she had seen. But soon, Jigoro Kano himself agreed to be her instructor. There were very few women at that time learning martial arts—most women were still encouraged to follow more traditional pursuits.

Keiko's mother and brother supported her because they believed she would end up marrying a judoka (judo expert). She surprised them by becoming a judo master herself!

In 1937, Keiko began teaching judo. She traveled between Japan and the United States, teaching and lecturing passionately about her beloved sport of judo. Years later, she settled in San Francisco, California, and became a U.S. citizen.

There was a separate ranking for women, no matter how skilled they were at judo. Only five levels of black belt achievement were recognized. Yet, men could work toward ten levels. Many people felt this was unfair. But Keiko never complained. She just kept training and teaching. In the 1960s, the attitude toward women began to shift. But it wasn't until 2011 that Keiko was finally awarded the highest rank in martial arts—the coveted tenth dan—with its rare red belt. She is the only woman to ever achieve that honor.

Her love and passion for judo never wavered or diminished. She taught for almost seventy years and received many awards for her dedication and achievements. In a physically demanding and combative sport, she always remained humble and graceful.

Keiko believed that the goal of judo was to learn to be gentle on the outside and strong on the inside. It's a trait she fully embodied throughout her long and amazing lifetime.

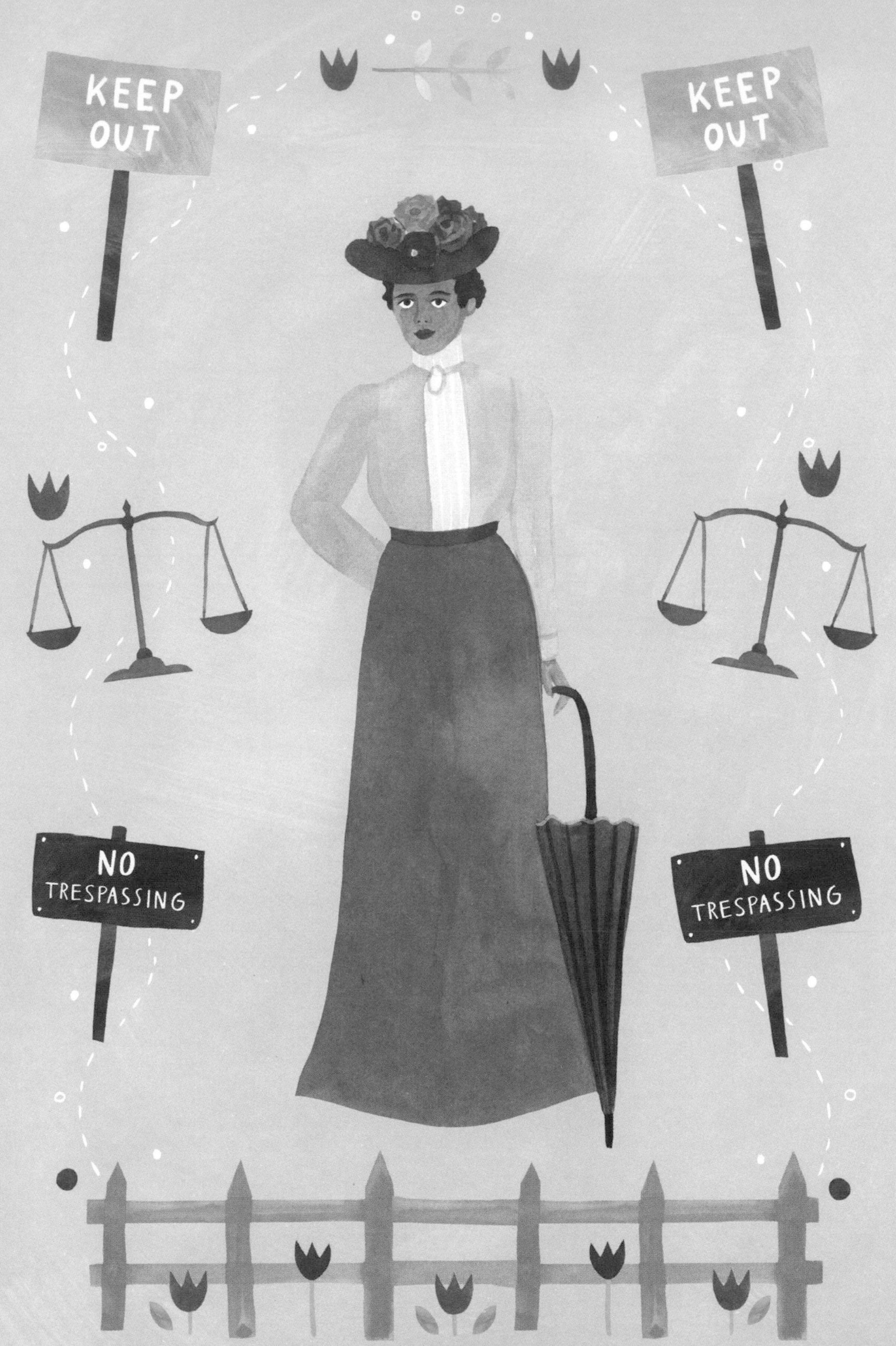
KEEP OUT
KEEP OUT
NO TRESPASSING
NO TRESPASSING

LYDA CONLEY

★ PROUD PROTECTOR ★

Lyda and her sisters were members of the Wyandot Nation. It was divided into two groups—one in Kansas and the other in Oklahoma.

Their parents encouraged them to pursue their education, and they did, which meant rowing across the Missouri River to attend Park College. Lyda graduated from the Kansas City School of Law in 1902. She was dedicated to representing Wyandot tribe members. But the biggest legal battle of her career would be her own.

In 1906, Kansas City was booming, and developers set their sights on a prime location—the Huron Cemetery. Lyda was horrified. This was where her parents and ancestors had been laid to rest. It was sacred burial ground! But the Wyandot tribe in Kansas didn't have legal control of the land. The group in Oklahoma did. And they wanted to sell.

With Lyda as their leader, the Conley sisters made it their mission to protect the cemetery. They built a crude six-foot-eight shack in the cemetery called "Fort Conley." The sisters moved in and took turns guarding the property twenty-four hours a day with their father's Civil War musket.

They also built a fence around the cemetery. It was torn down by law enforcement. They rebuilt it. It was torn down again. This went on for years—too many times to count.

In 1907, Lyda filed a legal petition to stop the sale of the cemetery. She lost. But she refused to give up.

In 1909, Lyda became the first Native American woman admitted to try a case before the United States Supreme Court.

She lost. But she wasn't defeated. The case attracted a lot of publicity and support—and that made Senator Charles Curtis take notice. In 1916, he passed a bill that protected the cemetery as a National Park. That kept the developers at bay but didn't end the battle. The controversy over who could decide the fate of the land continued for more than one hundred years. In 1971, the cemetery was listed on the National Register of Historic Places. The name was later changed to the Wyandot National Burying Ground, and it remains intact.

Lyda died on May 28, 1946, and was buried among her ancestors in the cemetery that she so proudly and valiantly protected.

MARGARET "MOLLY" TOBIN BROWN

★ ABSOLUTELY "UNSINKABLE" ★

Margaret grew up in Hannibal, Missouri, with her Irish immigrant parents and siblings. Maggie, as they called her, loved to climb the bluffs overlooking the Mississippi River and explore the nearby caves.

Her family was poor, and when she was thirteen years old, she took a job stripping leaves off tobacco plants in the Garth Tobacco Factory. It was boring work, but it gave her time to dream about traveling and having adventures when she grew up.

As soon as she got the chance, she followed her brother to a mining town in Colorado. Maggie's adventure had begun! She married a mining engineer, and in 1893 they struck it rich.

Maggie wanted to fit in with wealthy high-society women, so she hired tutors to teach her proper grammar and French. She bought new clothes and threw lavish parties.

But Maggie didn't fit in—and that wasn't a bad thing! She remembered what it was like to be poor. And she had seen how dangerous it was to work in the mines that had made her rich. She still threw parties—but now they had a purpose. Maggie would invite influential friends to charity balls to raise money to improve working conditions for miners. She also formed the Denver Women's Party in 1893 to fight for voting rights across the country.

Maggie's dream of traveling the world came true—and almost ended in disaster. In April 1912, she was headed back to the States from England on the maiden voyage of a new luxury ocean liner—the *Titanic*.

This modern, "unsinkable" ship hit an iceberg and began to sink.

Even though she was frightened, Maggie remained calm and helped others into Lifeboat 6. She grabbed an oar and helped row—and continued to reassure the others that they would be rescued.

And they were. The ship *Carpathia* picked them up. Their nightmarish ordeal was over.

But not forgotten.

Maggie wrote about her experiences on the *Titanic* for the *Denver Post*. She also raised money for the families of the survivors and helped erect a memorial in Washington, D.C. for those who had perished.

Others also wrote about her adventures and mistakenly called her "Molly" even though she never used that nickname. When a musical was written about her, "Molly" fit into the lyrics better than "Margaret" so the nickname stuck.

For the rest of her life, she helped others, even turning her house over to the American Red Cross in World War I to use as a temporary hospital.

In 1932, this flamboyant and outspoken woman was awarded the French Legion of Honor for her "overall good citizenship." Maggie *was* a good citizen—and so much more.

MARY EDWARDS WALKER

★ MEDAL OF HONOR WINNER ★

Mary didn't believe in following society's rules. In 1855, she became one of the first female doctors—when few women had careers outside the home. Then she did something even more outrageous. She wore bloomers! Instead of a constrictive corset and petticoat, she wore trousers under a knee-length skirt. People were shocked and appalled and she became the object of ridicule. Mary ignored the nasty comments and laughter and insisted that women should be allowed to wear comfortable clothes.

Mary had a difficult time as a doctor—nobody trusted a female physician, especially one wearing pants! But as the Civil War raged, she realized she could be of help to wounded soldiers. She moved to Washington, D.C. and tried to join the army as a surgeon, but was rejected. Never one to give up, Mary went to the battlefield anyway.

Again, the army refused to use her as a surgeon, so she found herself doing menial tasks like writing letters for the soldiers, taking temperatures, and changing bandages.

Finally, in 1863, she was appointed as the first female assistant U.S. Army surgeon. Mary made her own blue uniform—complete with pants and a stylish hat. She didn't wait for the wounded soldiers to be brought to the medical tent. Instead, she rode on horseback to the battlefields, frequently dodging bullets! She tended to soldiers on both sides of the conflict—if a soldier needed help, she was there to give it.

In 1864, her disregard for battle lines caught up with her, and she was caught by Confederate soldiers and imprisoned as a spy in Richmond, Virginia. Four months later, Army officers made a deal—a Confederate Army surgeon and Mary would be part of a prisoner exchange—and they were both released. It meant that the army finally saw her value as a surgeon, despite her gender and odd manner of dress.

When the war ended, Mary joined the celebration by reading the Declaration of Independence on the steps of Virginia's State Capitol.

In 1866, two things happened to Mary. President Andrew Johnson awarded her the Medal of Honor for her valor and courage during the Civil War—making her the only woman to ever receive this award. And she was arrested for wearing pants in public!

Mary spent the rest of her life writing and lecturing about women's rights. She believed every woman should be able to pursue her dreams and wear whatever she wanted while doing so!

MARY FIELDS

★ "STAGECOACH MARY" ★

Mary Fields never knew her exact birth date. When you are born into slavery, things like birthdays aren't important. As a young child, she was expected to work on the plantation. And she did—plowing the fields and growing stronger each passing season.

When slavery was abolished, Mary stayed to work on the plantation. By that time, she was known for making her own rules—and cigars! She wore an apron, which covered her men's trousers—and her gun. She was known as a crack shot and enjoyed shooting bottles for target practice.

When she was about fifty, she was hired to work at a convent in Montana. This gun-toting, rough-and-tumble woman must have been quite a sight among the nuns! Mary supervised the hired hands and the crew building a school for Native American children. She did laundry, tended the garden, and took care of hundreds of chickens. And she drove the convent supply wagon and stagecoach—which earned her the nickname "Stagecoach Mary."

One man refused to take orders from her, even though she was the boss. To settle matters, she challenged him to a gunfight. Guns blazed! Bullets flew!

He lost. She winged him, but he lived.

She won. But she lost her job.

Mary then opened a café and proved that she also had a softer side. She made it a point to feed everyone that walked through the door—whether they could pay her or not. She was a kind soul but a lousy businesswoman. Her café closed. She later reopened the café, but Mary didn't change her ways, and it soon closed again—this time for good.

In 1882, she started a new job—as a stagecoach driver for the United States Postal Service. Mary was not your typical mail carrier. She drove her route brandishing a bullwhip and her trusty gun!

During one blizzard, the icy road was too narrow and the snow too high for the stagecoach to pass. Mary simply heaved the mail sacks onto her mighty shoulders and trudged through the snow to make her deliveries.

Mary was well known in the town of Cascade for both her toughness and her kindness. Since she didn't know her birthdate, she'd celebrate twice a year, whenever the mood struck her. Children would get the day off school to join in the festivities.

When Mary died, the town held a huge funeral to mourn the loss—and celebrate the life—of a truly remarkable, one-of-a-kind woman.

MINNIE SPOTTED WOLF

★ MARVELOUS MARINE ★

Minnie grew up on a ranch on the Blackfeet Indian Reservation in northern Montana. She loved riding horses and being outdoors. Never one to shy away from hard work, she cut wood, mended fences, and herded cattle. She trained horses alongside her father. Minnie was as comfortable behind the wheel of a truck as she was on the back of a horse—whatever it took to get her where she was going!

She was eighteen years old when World War II began. Minnie felt a strong desire to serve her country and made the bold decision to join the U.S. Marine Corps. But when she went to enlist, the recruiter turned her down—telling her war was no place for a woman.

Minnie, disappointed, returned to ranching. Her patriotism grew stronger as the war raged on. Attitudes toward women in the military slowly changed, and in 1943, the Women's Reserve was established. It was the opportunity Minnie had been waiting for! Just after she signed up, tragedy struck. Her father died, and she was torn between fulfilling her dream of military service or staying home and helping out. Her mother and sisters told her the country needed her and she should follow her heart—and make them and the Blackfeet Nation proud.

And she did! Minnie became the first Native American woman to join the U.S. Marine Corps. Her years of hard work on the ranch paid off—helping her make it through the physically grueling boot camp. She was assigned to drive huge trucks—something else she had learned on the ranch. Minnie transported soldiers, equipment, and weapons. She also drove visiting officers around the base. Many of the male marines were skeptical of her at first, until she proved that not only could she keep up with them as an excellent driver, but she could also take apart an engine and put it back together again!

Minnie quickly earned the respect and admiration of her fellow marines, and she was featured in a dramatic four-page comic book included in *Calling All Girls* magazine, which was very popular with teen girls in the 1940s. It told the story of her background and her current accomplishments in the military.

After her time in the Marines, Minnie went to college, earned a degree, and taught for twenty-nine years, encouraging a new generation of children to pursue their dreams—just as she had.

ROSE FORTUNE

★ COURAGEOUS COP ★

Rose was born into slavery in Virginia. When she was ten years old, just after the Revolutionary War, she escaped with her family and fled to Canada. She eventually settled in the bustling seaport town of Annapolis Royal, Nova Scotia.

It was difficult for a woman, especially a black woman, to find work. But that didn't stop Rose. If no one would hire her, she'd start her own business. In 1825, she began toting suitcases in a wheelbarrow from the docks to hotels for arriving passengers. If anyone got in her way, she'd poke them with a stick!

But she was much more than a delivery person. Being a well-known figure on the docks, she was often asked to watch property, guard belongings, and patrol warehouses. Her reputation as being trustworthy and loyal soon grew—and so did her responsibilities. Rose bravely enforced curfews and kept an eye on unsavory characters. She also maintained order on the wharf, scolding children if they misbehaved.

Although it was never official, she was hailed as the first woman police officer in Canada. It was said she knew everyone—and everyone knew her.

Rose was easily recognizable by her outfit—which was captured in a watercolor painting around 1830. This stout, no-nonsense woman wore a man's heavy coat over a dress with a white apron—and a ruffled petticoat peeping out below it. She had work boots with heels, and a cap under a straw hat tied under her chin.

Rose always paid close attention to what was happening on the dock. And what she saw gave her the idea for a new business. Many travelers had to hurry to board ships on time—being late could mean waiting weeks for another one. Rose stepped in to help and created a "wake-up call" service. She'd go to the nearby inns and hotels and personally wake up passengers so they wouldn't miss their departure time.

Rose eventually traded her wheelbarrow for horse-drawn wagons to expand her baggage transportation business, which later became known as *Lewis Transfer*. Over the years she enlisted the help of her children and grandchildren—who kept the company going for over a hundred years.

Rose's legacy as an entrepreneur and keeper of the peace has been celebrated by the Association of Black Law Enforcers, who created a scholarship in her name—a fitting honor for a woman who was proud to serve and protect those in her beloved adopted seaport.

SUSAN LA FLESCHE PICOTTE

★ HEROIC HEALER ★

Susan was raised as part of the Omaha Nation of Nebraska during a time when the lives of the Plains Indians were rapidly changing. Her father was chief of the Omaha tribe, and her mother was the daughter of the first Army physician in Nebraska. They wanted their children to learn to live in both worlds, so they sent them to an English-speaking school. Susan was so young—and small—that she could take naps inside her lift-lid school desk! She was a curious child and a talented student.

Straddling two cultures wasn't easy, and one incident demonstrated the deep divide between them. An Indian woman became ill, and the local white doctor was sent for—but he refused to come. Susan watched the woman die. It had such a powerful impact on her, she dedicated her life to improving the health care for her people.

When she was fourteen, she attended the Elizabeth Institute for Young Ladies and later the Hampton Institute in Virginia—which once again placed her in a tug-of-war between new beliefs and lifestyles and her old traditions and heritage. But her success as a student gave her the confidence and courage to do something bold: apply to medical school. She was accepted by the Women's Medical College of Pennsylvania.

Susan graduated and returned home as the first Native American physician in the country. But that's when the hard work really began. Susan never turned down a patient—Indian or white. She had over 1,200 patients spread out over 450 square miles! That meant making house calls on horseback in all types of weather. Frequently the ride was so rough she arrived only to find a saddlebag full of broken thermometers and bottles. She endured snowstorms, blazing heat, and everything in between. But her patients always came before her own comfort or safety.

Not only did Susan tend to the sick, she also taught the importance of proper hygiene and preventive care. She witnessed firsthand the devastating effects of alcoholism and fought tirelessly to combat it by educating people about addiction.

Despite everything, she was paid only $500 a year, while male doctors made at least ten times more.

Susan married, had children, and still continued to work as a doctor.

Finally, in 1913, two years before her death, the Susan La Flesche Picotte Memorial Hospital was built in Walthill, Nebraska, honoring the woman who devoted her life to healing wounds—in both bodies and attitudes.

SYBIL LUDINGTON

 ★ HEROIC HORSEWOMAN ★

Like most sixteen-year-old girls in the 1770s, Sybil Ludington was expected to do a lot of ordinary chores. She had to watch over her younger siblings. Cook. Clean. Sew. Help around the farm. Tend to her beloved horse, Star.

She also had one not-so-ordinary chore: guard duty.

Her father, Colonel Henry Ludington, had worked alongside General George Washington at the beginning of the Revolutionary War when the colonists wanted to break ties with Great Britain and form their own country. He later became the militia commander for troops in New York. The British offered a reward for his capture—dead or alive.

Sybil was determined to keep him safe. One night, she realized the house was surrounded by British soldiers and the family was in danger! She quickly gave all of her brothers and sisters lighted candles and had them walk through all the rooms of the house—and in front of the windows. From the outside, it looked like the house was heavily protected. It would be foolish to attack.

And they didn't.

On the stormy night of April 26, 1777, Colonel Ludington got word that the British were burning the town of Danbury, where most of the troop's precious supplies were stored. He needed to plan a counterattack. But he also needed someone to ride over the dangerous and rugged roads to warn the militia members of an impending attack and tell them to meet at his farmhouse by daybreak.

He needed someone brave. Someone willing to risk death for the cause. That someone was young Sybil.

Mounting her horse, Star, Sybil rode over forty miles, evading highwaymen and enemy soldiers. She raced through towns shouting a warning that the British were burning Danbury. Village bells rang out to alert the militia and send them to the Ludingtons' farmhouse.

When Sybil finally returned home at dawn—weary and rain-soaked—she was met by over four hundred men who had answered her call for help. Because of her brave and historic ride, the patriots were able to force the British troops out of the area.

Sybil was not the only patriot to dash through the night to shout the warning "The British are coming!" Paul Revere is famous for his midnight ride, even though it was half as long and less dangerous than Sybil's!

BIBLIOGRAPHY

Allen, Nancy Kelly. *Barreling over Niagara Falls*. Gretna: Pelican Publishing Company, 2013.

Alter, Judy. *Extraordinary Women of the American West*. New York: Children's Press, 1999.

Anema, Durlynn. *Ynes Mexia: Botanist and Adventurer*. Greensboro: Morgan Reynolds Publishing, 2005.

Baker, Daniel B., editor. *Explorers and Discoverers of the World*. Washington, D.C.: Gale Research Inc., 1999.

Barnes, Susan. "A Visit with the Shark Lady: Dr. Eugenie Clark." *Odyssey* 18, no. 5 (May/June 2009): 42–43.

Beckner, Chrisanne. *100 African-Americans Who Changed History*. Milwaukee: World Almanac Library, 2005.

Birchfield, D. L., general editor, *The Encyclopedia of North American Indians*. New York: Marshall Cavendish, 1997.

Black, Dennis H. *Profiles of Valor: Iowa's Medal of Honor Recipients of the Civil War*. Des Moines: Lexicon, 2010.

Borden, Louise and Kroger, Mary Kay. *Fly High! The Story of Bessie Coleman*. New York: Margaret K. McElderry, 2001.

Branzei, Sylvia. *Rebel in a Dress: Cowgirls*. Philadelphia: RP Kids, 2011.

Briggs, Carole S. *Women Space Pioneers*. Minneapolis: Lerner Publications Company, 2005.

Brown, Tami Lewis. *Soar, Elinor!* New York: Farrar Straus and Giroux, 2010.

Butts, Ed. *She Dared: True Stories of Heroines, Scoundrels, and Renegades*. Toronto: Tundra Books, 2005.

Caravantes, Peggy. *Petticoat Spies: Six Women Spies of the Civil War*. Greensboro: Morgan Reynolds Publishers, Inc., 2002.

Carpenter, Suzanne. "Confederate Spy." *Cobblestone* 20, no. 9 (December 1999): 18.

Casey, Susan. *Women Heroes of the American Revolution: 20 Stories of Espionage, Sabotage, Defiance, and Rescue*. Chicago: Chicago Review Press, 2015.

Champagne, Duane. *Native America: Portrait of the Peoples*. Detroit: Visible Ink, 1994.

Cummins, Julie. *Women Daredevils*. New York: Dutton Children's Books, 2008.

Cummins, Julie. *Women Explorers*. New York: Dial Books for Young Readers, 2012.

Davis, Linda M. "One Small Step." *Aviation History* 19, no. 6 (July 2009): 15.

Delano, Marfe Ferguson. *American Heroes*. Washington, D.C.: National Geographic, 2005.

Down, Susan Brophy. *Irena Sendler: Bringing Life to Children of the Holocaust*. New York: Crabtree Publishing Company, 2012.

Eidelman, Tamara. "The Extraordinary Destiny of an 'Ordinary' Woman." *Russian Life* 46, no.3 (May/June 2003): 19.

Ellison, Lillian. *The Fabulous Moolah: First Goddess of the Squared Circle*. New York: Regan Books, 2002.

Farquhar, Michael. *A Treasury of Foolishly Forgotten Americans: Pirates, Skinflints, Patriots, and Other Colorful Characters Stuck in the Footnotes of History*. New York: Penguin Books, 2008.

Feldman, Heather. *Valentina Tereshkova: The First Woman in Space*. New York: The Rosen Publishing Company, Inc., 2003.

Ferris, Jeri. *Native American Doctor: The Story of Susan La Flesche Picotte*. Minneapolis: Carolrhoda Books, 1991.

Freeling, Elisa. "When Grandma Gatewood Hikes the Appalachian Trail." *Sierra* 87, no. 6 (November/December 2002): 26.

Freese, Gene Scott. *Hollywood Stunt Performers, 1910s–1970s: A Biographical Dictionary*. Jefferson: McFarland & Company, Inc. Publishers, 2014.

Furbee, Mary Rodd. *Outrageous Women of Colonial America*. San Francisco: Jossey-Bass, 2001.

Furbee, Mary Rodd. *Outrageous Women of the American Frontier*. New York: Jon Wiley & Sons, 2002.

Gilliland, Ben. *100 People Who Made History*. New York: DK, 2012.

Gourley, Catherine. *Gidgets and Women Warriors: Perceptions of Women in the 1950s and 1960s*. Minneapolis: Twenty-First Century Books, 2008.

Gourley, Catherine. *Rosie and Mrs. America: Perceptions of Women in the 1930s and 1940s*. Minneapolis: Twenty-First Century Books, 2008.

Grace, N. B. *Women in Space*. Chanhassen: The Child's World, 2007.

Gregory, Mollie. *Stuntwomen: The Untold Hollywood Story*. Lexington: University Press of Kentucky, 2015.

Grimes, Nikki. *Talkin' about Bessie: The Story of Aviator Elizabeth Coleman*. New York: Orchard Books, 2002.

Gueldenpfennig, Sonia. *Women in Space Who Changed the World*. New York: The Rosen Publishing Group, Inc., 2012.

Hanbury-Tenison, Robin, editor. *The Great Explorers*. New York: Thames & Hudson, 2010.

Harness, Cheryl. *Mary Walker Wears the Pants: The True Story of the Doctor, Reformer, and Civil War Hero*. Chicago: Albert Whitman & Company, 2013.

Harness, Cheryl. *Rabble Rousers: 20 Women Who Made a Difference*. New York: Dutton Children's Books, 2003.

Haven, Kendall. *Amazing American Women: 40 Fascinating 5-Minute Reads*. Englewood: Libraries Unlimited, Inc., 1995.

Hearst, Michael. *Extraordinary People*. San Francisco: Chronicle Books, 2015.

Horn, Robert. "No Mountain Too High for Her—Junko Tabei Defied Japanese Views of Women to Become Expert Climber." *Sports Illustrated* (29 April 1996).

January, Brendan. *Amazing Explorers: A Book of Answers for Kids*. New York: John Wiley & Sons, Inc., 2001.

Jensen, Dean. *Queen of the Air: A True Story of Love & Tragedy at the Circus*. New York: Crown Publishers, 2013.

Juettner, Bonnie. *100 Native Americans Who Changed American History*. Milwaukee: World Almanac Library, 2005.

Keenan, Sheila. *Scholastic Encyclopedia of Women in the United States*. New York: Scholastic Inc., 1996.

Kenyon, J. Michael. "Mildred Burke...She Never Met Her Match." *Los Angeles Times*, April 17, 1981.

Kimmel, Elizabeth Cody. *Ladies First: 40 Daring American Women Who Were Second to None*. Washington, D.C.: National Geographic Society, 2006.

Klobuchar, Lisa. *Elizabeth Blackwell: With Profiles of Elizabeth Garrett Anderson and Susan La Flesche Picotte*. Chicago: World Book Inc., 2007.

Krohn, Katherine. *Wild West Women*. Minneapolis: Lerner Publications Company, 2006.

Krull, Kathleen, and Kathryn Hewitt. *Lives of the Explorers: Discoveries, Disasters (and What the Neighbors Thought)*. New York: Houghton Mifflin Harcourt, 2014.

Landau, Elaine. *Heroine of the Titanic: The Real Unsinkable Molly Brown*. New York: Clarion Books, 2001.

Langley, Wanda. *Women of the Wind: Early Women Aviators*. Greensboro: Morgan Reynolds Publishing, 2006.

Ledbetter, Suzann. *Shady Ladies: Nineteen Surprising and Rebellious American Women*. New York: A Tom Doherty Associates Book, 2006.

Leen, Jeff. *The Queen of the Ring: Sex, Muscles, Diamonds, and the Making of an American Legend*. New York: Atlantic Monthly Press, 2009.

Letchworth, Beverly J. "Annette the Mermaid." *Cricket* 43, no. 9 (July/August 2016): 23–25.

Lohse, Joyce B. *Unsinkable: The Molly Brown Story*. Palmer Lake: Filter Press, LLC., 2006.

Lopes, Rosaly. *The Volcano Adventure Guide*. Cambridge: Cambridge University Press, 2005.

Macy, Sue. *Winning Ways: A Photohistory of American Women in Sports*. New York: Henry Holt and Company, 1996.

Madden, Annette. *In Her Footsteps: 101 Remarkable Black Women from the Queen of Sheba to Queen Latifah*. Berkeley: Conari Press, 2000.

Mahon, Elizabeth Kerri. *Scandalous Women: The Lives and Loves of History's Most Notorious Women*. New York: Penguin Books, 2001.

"Marine Biologist Eugenie Clark Remembered as Passionate Shark Advocate." *All Things Considered*. National Public Radio. February 26, 2015. Radio.

Markey, Kevin. *100 Most Important Women of the 20th Century*. Des Moines: Meredith Publishing Group, 1998.

Martin, Paul. *Secret Heroes: Everyday Americans Who Shaped Our World*. New York: Harper Collins Publishers, 2012.

McGovern, Ann. *Shark Lady: True Adventures of Eugenie Clark*. New York: Scholastic, 1978.

McGraw, Eliza. "A Rebel to the Core." *American History* 38, no. 2 (June 2003): 14.

Millar, Ruth Wright. *Saskatchewan Heroes & Rogues*. Regina: Coteau Books, 2004.

Miller, John, editor. *Legends*. Novato: New World Library, 1998.

Mitchell, Saundra. *They Did What? 50 Unbelievable Women and Their Fascinating (and True!) Stories*. New York: Puffin Books, 2016.

Montgomery, Ben. *Grandma Gatewood's Walk: The Inspiring Story of the Woman Who Saved the Appalachian Trail*. Chicago: Chicago Review Press, 2014.

Montgomery, Ben. "Train Blazer." *Rodale's Organic Life* 2, no. 4 (July/August 2016): 46.

Moss, Marissa. *The Bravest Woman in America*. New York: Tricycle Press, 2011.

Newby, Eric. *A Book of Traveler's Tales*. New York: Viking, 1985.

Niven, Jennifer. *Ada Blackjack: A True Story of Survival in the Arctic*. New York: Hyperion, 2003.

Nivola, Claire A. *Life in the Ocean: The Story of Oceanographer Sylvia Earle*. New York: Farrar Straus Giroux, 2012.

Otake, Tomoko. "Junko Tabei: The First Woman Atop the World." *The Japan Times*, May 27, 2012.

Rappaport, Doreen. *We Are the Many: A Picture Book of American Indians*. New York: Harper Collins, 2002.

Rappoport, Ken. *Ladies First: Women Athletes Who Made a Difference*. Atlanta: Peachtree Publishers, 2009.

Reese, Diana. "Grandma Gatewood Survived Domestic Violence to Walk the Appalachian Trail Alone at 67." *The Washington Post*, January 5, 2015.

Riddles, Libby. *Storm Run: The Story of the First Woman to Win the Iditarod*. Seattle: Sasquatch Books, 2002.

Ridley, Glynis. *The Discovery of Jeanne Baret: A Story of Science, the High Seas, and the First Woman to Circumnavigate the Globe*. New York: Broadway Paperbacks, 2010.

Roehm, Michelle. *Girls Who Rocked the World 2*. Hillsboro: Beyond Words Publishing, Inc., 2000.

Rooney, Frances. *Extraordinary Women Explorers*. Toronto: Second Story Press, 2005.

Ross, Michael Elsohn. *A World of Her Own: 24 Amazing Women Explorers and Adventurers*. Chicago: Chicago Review Press, 2014.

Rubin, Susan Goldman. *Irena Sendler and the Children of the Warsaw Ghetto*. New York: Holiday House, 2011.

Rubin, Susan Goldman. *Margaret Bourke-White: Her Pictures Were Her Life*. New York: Harry N. Abrams, Inc., Publishers, 1999.

Ruffin, Frances E. *"Unsinkable" Molly Brown*. New York: Powerkids Press, 2002.

Silvis, Randall. *North of Unknown: Mina Hubbard's Extraordinary Expedition Into the Labrador Wilderness*. Guilford: The Lyons Press, 2005.

Smith, Elinor. *Aviatrix*. Thorndike: Thorndike Press, 1981.

Snow, Richard F. "Belle Boyd." *American Heritage* 31, no. 2 (February/March 1980): 94–95.

Stamaty, Mark Alan. *Alia's Mission: Saving the Books of Iraq*. New York: Alfred A. Knopf, 2004.

Thimmesh, Catherine. *Girls Think of Everything*. Boston: Houghton Mifflin Co., 2000.

Thimmesh, Catherine. *The Sky's the Limit: Stories of Discovery by Women and Girls*. Boston: Houghton Mifflin Co., 2002.

Van Allsburg, Chris. *Queen of the Falls*. New York: Houghton Mifflin Books for Children, 2011.

Vaughn, Marcia. *Irena's Jar of Secrets*. New York: Lee & Low Books, 2011.

Von Berge, Emily. "The Mysterious Kate Warne." *Hopscotch* 26, no. 5 (February/March 2015): 26–27.

Weatherford, Doris. *American Women's History: An A to Z of People, Organizations, Issues, and Events*. New York: Prentice Hall, 1994.

Whitley, Sharon. "Lillian Boyer Remembers Days Winging It as Aerial Daredevil." *The San Diego Union*, March 24, 1987.

Wilner, Barry. *The Best Auto Racers of All Time*. North Mankato: Abdo Publishing, 2015.

Winkler, H. Donald. *Stealing Secrets: How a Few Daring Women Deceived Generals, Impacted Battles, and Altered the Course of the Civil War*. Naperville: Sourcebooks, Inc., 2010.

Winter, Jeanette. *The Librarian of Basra: A True Story from Iraq*. New York: Harcourt, Inc., 2005.

Winter, Jonah. *Wild Women of the Wild West*. New York: Holiday House, 2011.

Yoshikawa, Mai. "Mountain Queen Not Done Yet: Junko Tabei." *The Japan Times*, February 25, 2003.

Zanjani, Sally. *Mine of Her Own: Women Prospectors in the American West 1850–1950*. Lincoln: University of Nebraska Press, 1997.

Zeinert, Karen. *Those Remarkable Women of the American Revolution*. Brookfield: Millbrook Press, 1996.

Zhuelin, Peter. *Annie Londonderry's Extraordinary Ride Around the World on Two Wheels*. New York: Citadel Press, 2007.

Zhuelin, Peter. "Chasing Annie." *Bicycling* 46, no. 4 (May 2005): 64–69.

INDEX OF THE
WOMEN WHO DARED

A

ADVENTURERS, 31
Anning, Mary, 61
Ayettey, Beatrice, 37

B

Baker, Alia Muhammad, 73
Baret, Jeanne, 49
Blackjack, Ada, 33
Blanchard, Sophie, 26
Bourke-White, Margaret, 58
Boyd, Belle, 78
Boyer, Lillian, 14
Broadwick, Georgia "Tiny", 10
Brown, Anna Olga Albertina, 1
Brown, Margaret "Molly" Tobin, 94
Burke, Mildred, 22

C

Chadwick, Florence, 9
Clark, Dr. Eugenie, 41
Coleman, Bessie, 5
Conley, Lyda, 93

D

DAREDEVILS, vii

E

Earle, Sylvia, 66
Ellison, Mary Lillian, 18

F

Fields, Mary, 98
Fletcher, Joan Bamford, 50
Fortune, Rose, 102
Fukuda, Keiko, 90

G

Gatewood, Emma "Grandma", 38
Gibson, Helen, 13

H

Hattan, Ella, 82
Hillary, Barbara, 34
Hubbard, Mina, 62

J

July, Johanna, 86

K

Kellerman, Annette, 74
Kopchovsky, Annie
    "Londonderry" Cohen, 77

L

Leitzel, Lillian, 17
Lewis, Ida, 46
Lopes, Rosaly, 65
Ludington, Sybil, 106

M

Mexia, Ynes, 69
Muldowney, Shirley, 25

P

Picotte, Susan La Flesche, 105

R

REBELS, 71
Riddles, Libby, 54
Riggs, Lillian, 57

S

Sarras, Ferminia, 45
Sendler, Irena, 85
Smith, Elinor, 6
Stringfield, Bessie, 81

T

Tabei, Junko, 53
Taylor, Annie Edson, 2
Tereshkova, Valentina, 29

W

Walker, Mary Edwards, 97
Warne, Kate, 89
Wirth, May Emmeline, 21
Wolf, Minnie Spotted, 101
Workman, Fanny Bullock, 42

ABOUT THE AUTHOR

Linda Skeers is the author of several critically acclaimed children's books. She also teaches picture book writing workshops, including sessions on writing humor for kids. She lives in Iowa. Visit her at www.lindaskeers.com.

ABOUT THE ILLUSTRATOR

Livi Gosling has always been inspired by powerful, creative women. Learning about these amazing women and hearing their stories has been wonderful. She is so glad that their stories are being shared. Livi studied illustration in Cornwall and currently lives in Hertfordshire village in the UK. Visit her at www.livigosling.co.uk

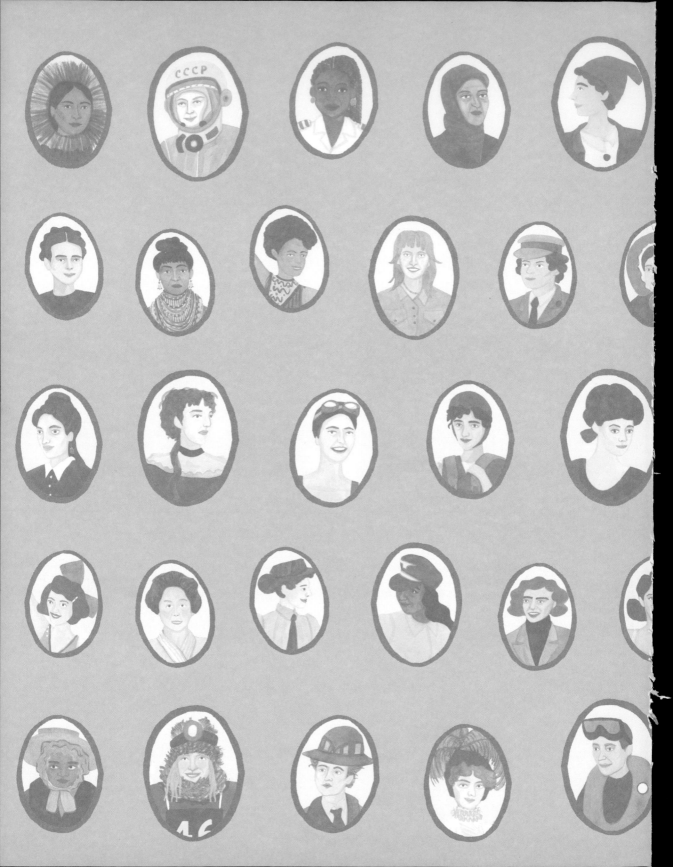